UNCOVERING THE VOICE

UNCOVERING
THE VOICE

A Path towards Catharsis in the Art of Singing

VALBORG WERBECK-SVÄRDSTRÖM

with an afterword by Dr. E. Kolisko

translated by P. Luborsky

ANTHROPOSOPHIC PRESS

RUDOLF STEINER PRESS
LONDON

First Edition: Rudolf Steiner Press, 1980
Second Edition: Rudolf Steiner Press, 1985
Translated from the German *Die Schule der Stimmenthüllung*,
published by Philosophisch-Anthroposophischer Verlag,
Dornach 1975

CONTENTS

Preface to the German Edition   1

Foreword   17

Chapter One   30
INTRODUCTION

Chapter Two   56
MUSICAL SOUND AND THE SOUNDS OF SPEECH:
TWO ESSENTIALLY DISTINCT WORLDS

Chapter Three   74
FIRST PHASE: DIRECTION OF THE SOUND

Chapter Four   91
SECOND PHASE: EXPANSION

Chapter Five   112
THIRD PHASE: REFLECTION OF THE SOUND

Chapter Six   128
THE SOUNDS OF SPEECH, OR
THE REFLECTION OF THE WORD

Chapter Seven   145
THE PHYSIOLOGY OF THE TONGUE

Chapter Eight   166
THE ART OF BREATHING

Chapter Nine   182
CONCLUSION

Chapter Ten   198
ON THE FORGOTTEN SENSE OF LISTENING

Afterword   202
PHYSIOLOGICAL AND THERAPEUTIC
CONSIDERATIONS (Dr. Eugen Kolisko)

Translator's Note   220

PREFACE TO THE GERMAN EDITION

The present work, *Uncovering the Voice,* is the result of study and research extending from 1910/1911, through the first world war, and on into the thirties. In 1938, when the first edition appeared in Breslau, the situation in Germany was already such that all free spiritual life was suppressed. As a work nourished from the springs of Rudolf Steiner's spiritual science, it naturally could no longer find any ground to stand on. The book was passed from hand to hand among students and interested persons. During the second world war, dissemination of the book was even less possible, and the post-war collapse brought with it the loss of all remaining copies.

Now the work is brought out again in very different times. The author, at her advanced age, is unable to rewrite it. The reader is asked to take this into account; the book is now printed in unaltered form.

As it happens, this is quite justifiable; for though the intervening decades may have seen a number of meritorious investigations into singing, there is to our knowledge none among the more significant works that proceeds from a viewpoint similar to the one taken here. The majority of these investigations seek to delve with ever greater precision into the physiological basis of vocal art. It is also well known that even the practical path of study cannot go on without a psychological view of the matter; but the *spiritual* side is difficult to approach without a science of the spirit.

It is precisely from this point that we proceed here — that is, from the actual encounter with the spiritual entelechy of tone itself. From here we descend into the soul, and finally into the bodily sphere of practical exercise, with the various muscular functions which must be educated to differentiated use — for example, in order to achieve perfect articulation.

It is obvious that from this point of view the higher spiritual-soul plane must develop in a special way; thus it need merely be indicated here that as he progresses from step to step, the student must experience his whole being engaged in a process of metamorphosis, in perfect yet strict harmony with his practical attainments.

'Holistic' processes are spoken of again and again as a pedagogical ideal in all fields; however, this is not so easy to achieve. For example, a mere physiological co-ordination of a number of muscle complexes achieved through one or another functional conception derived from breathing exercises — this can never make an integral whole, no matter how comprehensively it may be designed; for the relation of this process to the soul, and above all to the spirit, is lacking.

Since in such a case the real level on which the human being exists is not touched at all, the vibrations set off flow on a subordinate plane, and what we call the Creative does not come into play at all. (Psychological picture-images also provide only a partial aspect, as stimulating, fruitful, and even indispensable as they are.)

The fundamental conclusions presented in this book were all thoroughly discussed with Rudolf Steiner, and in January 1924 they were all recognised and authorised by him as a spiritual-scientifically oriented school of singing for our times. Despite its clarity as a system and the exact methods flowing from this, the work can also be seen as presenting the very personal path of development of an important artistic personality. In other words, this school is capable of — indeed, disposed towards — further development in different directions.

It was the author's wish that a student of this school might introduce the new edition. Therefore, let a few considerations be added by a member of a younger generation, in relation to the work of this school in the present cultural situation.

It is interesting to note that a number of discoveries, which the author puts forth as still rather hypothetical, have been confirmed in the meantime by physiological research.

The most fundamental of these is no doubt the recognition of the self-vibration of the vocal cords. This does away with a crudely mechanistic 19th century conception which regarded the larynx as a sort of bagpipes blown by air from the lungs.

We greet such a discovery with relief, for that obsolete conception has had most injurious effects. As early as 1868 the great Swedish singer Jenny Lind, writing in a letter about her art of singing, said that true singing had been lost: all that one heard now as singing was really a form of screaming or speaking; even in Italy the real tradition could no longer be found.

One may find it surprising to hear such statements about a decline in the art of singing in a time which, to our view, seems still filled with health and strength. It should not be forgotten that soon after Goethe's death, a current of thought made new headway which already in the 18th century had depicted man as a machine. In between came the spiritually powerful, though relatively short intermezzo of German Idealism, which had such a broad cultural effect throughout Europe. The phenomenon of German Idealism must seem all the more miraculous to us the further we leave it behind, and yet it could do no more than interrupt

3

the above-mentioned materialistic stream. The latter leads, girded with stronger natural-scientific foundations, to the climax of materialism in the last third of the 19th century, bringing the incalculably destructive consequences of which the whole world today bears evidence.

At the time when Jenny Lind made the statement quoted above, this development was already in full swing. And so it seems important to realise now that it is not a matter of indifference whether the thoughts we form about something correspond to reality or not. Each muscle movement will be different according to how the thought enters in as motivation. Ultimately it is the innermost disposition which has the most delicate effect — on the breathing process, for example, making it noticeably heavier or lighter. At that time physiological thinking seized upon the processes of singing. All physiological functions were investigated. The invention of the laryngoscope by Garcia (1855) gave impetus to this. Of course we do not mean to say anything against the need for such research — it corresponds completely to our state of consciousness; but we are beginning today to recognise that it has brought a marked coarsening and distortion into our ideas about the subtle processes involved in song and speech, with consequences which are now quite obvious.

The phenomenon of the self-vibration of the vocal cords, which cannot be described further here, by itself can awaken us to the untold complexity of the preconditions necessary for singing and speaking in the physical organism alone. The ever more exact investigation of the muscle groups involved and their functioning shows us an astounding network of interconnections. For example, it appears that to manifest a true singing voice, something hard to imagine is required: simultaneous extension and contraction in the vocal cords themselves. A bewildering network of mutually contradictory muscle movements plays about the organ of song in absolutely breath-taking equilibristics. Any simplification in our way of thinking about these processes causes a coarsening, introduces decadence; for here, simplification mean imbalance. What a parable is offered here, even when we direct our gaze to the interaction of physical forces alone — a parable which leads us towards the profoundest knowledge of the human being!

Another discovery that seems important to us is the law that lung volume is inversely proportional to diaphragm muscle-tone. This throws light on the very first conversation between the author and Rudolf Steiner, and on many other parts of the book.

Lastly, we can refer to those studies that regard speech, ontologically, as a later, separated part derived from the realm of song and music. They see it as a sort of turning from within outward, from the ear to the eye, and can show the two domains to be qualitatively different even into their physical basis. The reader may look into the literature on this subject.

Thus it can be hoped that the purely mechanistic-physiological approach to song and speech — phenomena so eminently based in the realm of spirit and soul — is nearing its end.

One can see a sign of this in the sensitive understanding with which people once again approach the imaginative language of the old Italian school, and even admire the accuracy and felicity of its mode of expression. If it should prove possible to win back consciously what an instinctive knowledge dealt with unconsciously, then the whole state of affairs will no longer be the same; it will have changed, and will call forth other profound consequences of which we can as yet have no inkling.

At the same time the situation is changing along with the

altered structure of society. In our times, such a new attainment can only be the collective spiritual property of all, and not the privilege of the few, the specially gifted. What has been acquired anew must be embodied as a health-giving cultural impulse, especially for the entire education of the youth. That such thoughts are not utopian, we can see from the amazing precedent set at so many schools in Hungary through the forceful impulse of Zoltán Kodály. These methods will most certainly work to the benefit and health of the coming generation of the Hungarian people if they are consistently practised for a sufficient length of time. However, as long as our form of education remains so totally deficient it is likely that no thorough renewal will take hold, in which case decadence must take its relentless course, even in purely physiological terms (general phonaesthenia, etc.)

Our education must be called inadequate because it does not come to terms with the unprecedented complexity of modern social structure, to which living conditions subject us now. As a result, a person is not in the position to assert himself as a complete personality against the dissolving and crushing forces. He loses his equilibrium in many respects and finds himself sliding down the steep path towards becoming a faceless particle of the masses, prey for manipulation. We shall return to this all-embracing problem later.

This point in time seems particularly appropriate for the new edition out of a variety of reasons.

When we look at the musical situation of the present, we can perceive a turning point in the work of the leading composers since the fifties. After the possibilities of twelve-tone composition, in its different serial applications and procedures, had been thoroughly exhausted, it became apparent that this was not a new beginning, but a final phase of the past development of music. One of the leading composers of the avant garde (Pierre Boulez) speaks thus: in following these ways to their logical conclusion, there comes a time when the composer's personality is finally completely extinguished. Beyond such a void one sets out to find new ways for musical sound to crystallise. Now the direction is reversed, as it were: it is no longer the centre seeking for expression of its subjective self; rather, the sound is 'sucked in' from the periphery, out of the objective sphere. This process can hardly be described in words. Those acquainted with the work of Rudolf Steiner will recognise this transformation from point into sphere as a goal inherent in application of his *Philosophy of Freedom*. Steiner comments on this process in one of his lectures (of November 23, 1923):

'We stand within the sphere of the etheric world. We can no longer doubt the lawfulness of this cosmic ether-sphere when we have grasped thinking as it is presented in the *Philosophy of Freedom....* Just as in our ordinary thinking we stretch mental feelers outwards, so in such thinking — which experiences itself in itself — we continually stretch inward into ourselves. We become the object, an object to ourselves.... And in the process of this powerful grasping of the self, it comes about that we burst our own skin.'

If, at present, tone masses of varying concentration are the principle field of development, it seems justified to say — as many have done — that 'the individual tone is no longer of interest'.

Here it seems to us that an error is creeping in. For an ear exploring a new realm of sound, there is a great danger that it could find a changeling foisted on it in the form of *noise* (cf. the fascinating effect of 'musique concrete').

But if the inner ear has been soundly schooled in the tradition of Western music, it will be able to discriminate with great certainty at this threshold. Outer sound and

7

noise lie on the same plane as all mere sensory stimuli. They only excite the nerve endings. This age, which sucks dry our inner life, tends to use this nerve excitation as a kind of stimulant, in this case introduced not with drugs but directly through the sense of hearing. It gives the passive, empty soul an illusory sense of life. Ultimately, however, noise stimulation, like all outward stimulants, leads to total enervation, devastation of the soul — or more plainly, to dead boredom.

On the other hand, contact with the essence of tone, even in its most delicate expression (indeed, perhaps precisely there) penetrates deeply and enlivens us. The many experiments in which sound is distorted into noise may actually serve as a most useful preparation, since they teach us to recognise just what is *not* tone. And in the end, the pendulum will swing back again, and the longing for the revelation of the essence of tone will grow as overpowering as the desert-wanderer's thirst for a drink of clear, pure water. In fact, this interval of 'abstinence' might help us to achieve a completely new level of tone-experience — a prospect which awakens hope. In this regard we take a basically positive stance towards the experiment of our times, at least to the extent that it does not degenerate into destructive philistinism. Here again, the prime virtue to strive for would be the power of discrimination.

The experience of musical sound can only become real to us when it comes out of an *inner* hearing; and this presupposes a great intensification of our soul life. The nature of the times makes this an imperative demand. However, this heightening of auditory experience can only be achieved through careful cultivation of the musical tradition, beginning in childhood; and this means some form of active involvement with music. As we no longer have a society divided into different classes — an arrangement which in its time was capable of giving the growing youth a sufficient social education to meet life in his particular circumstances, this demand has long been a valid one for all levels of society. Since today the individual is necessarily isolated, it follows that each person has a right to an education that nurtures his individual needs. Our educational system has neglected the measures necessary for this, and the consequence in the sphere of musical culture is an increasing passivity of the hearing process (i.e., the will-aspect of auditory perception slackens). This draws after it the familiar and sad consequence that public interest is missing in contemporary musical concerns; and the source of this evil lies less in a lack of interest than in a simple lack of ability.

This incapacity, however, threatens to turn into something actively negative. That is, music tends more and more to be judged according to the feelings it stimulates, the effect it produces. The auditory process involves just the surface, the noise component of tone-phenomena. The inner dimension, our actual experience, is lost, and with it the significance of the evolution of Western music — for this runs parallel to the process of individuation. This loss in regard to inner hearing is in fact synonymous with the first stage of musical barbarism.

Our actual cultural plight still largely escapes popular awareness, and we continue onward under the worst illusions about these matters. It is no longer hard to see how the vicious circle comes into being: technical invention — decline of forces of individuality — craving for surrogates for their loss, satisfied by inundation of new technical inventions.

It is simply necessary to create a corresponding equivalent for the strengthening of the personality forces — today this is already one of the ABC's of popular psychology. Yet we have not faced this demand fully.

9

Such a strengthening can hardly be achieved except through active involvement in the various arts (see Rudolf Steiner's basic lecture 'Technology and Art,' December 28, 1914). However, traditional application of artistic means is not enough. A definite effort must be made to deepen our relation to art, otherwise it will be swept away by the current of technology. In reality, this robs it of its very most significant power: J.S. Bach spoke simply of 'recreation (re-creation) of the soul' as the purpose of music.

To bring the deepening needed in the field of singing, this school now enters in; and as its first task, it sets out explicitly in search of the lost integrity of the sung tone. The true musical sound having been found, it can be united with the formative force of the sounds of speech. In this process, each tone will be experienced more and more as a being, which one must approach with reverence if one hopes to share in its beneficial society. It could be compared to a wise man who, sensing a disrespectful attitude, locks up his treasures in himself. On the other hand, the power of the sung syllable is so deepened and strengthened through this union that the vocal literature of the past pales in comparison, despite all its perfection and beauty. A dimension of depth now begins to sound through which almost reminds us of the magical effects reported in the myths of ancient bards.

What we are experiencing in contemporary musical creation is a clear change in the relation of tone and word. Up till now, a connection was always more or less maintained, through the emotional content of a poem, for example; now this is dissolving. This need not absolutely be seen as a sign of disintegration; on its positive side, it enables us to experience the sounds of speech more intensely. The individuality of these sounds begins to interest us. They take on an immense richness of inner colour; they can even distil themselves into hieroglyphs of cosmic realities. If this deepening comes about in the right manner, then the familiar way of setting texts to music will fall away of itself. For example, songs with the melody repeated in each verse will take precedence over those composed with a continuous melody. In such fashion this change will yield quite a few interesting results.

One could speak similarly about what tone is able to reveal. Here, a change was felt quite early on. The young Stravinsky, for example, experienced the world of tone as one so unearthly and pure that it seemed to him almost a sacrilege to use it for the expression of human feelings. This sense has grown stronger today. Tones enter less and less into the world of human emotions, whether smaller or greater; and all the efforts of former times in this direction will seem to us a rather remarkable process of adapting music, of macrocosmic origin, to the narrow confines of the microcosm. Now this connection appears to be loosening. The world of tones and that of the speech sounds retreat into their primordial realms, challenging us, as it were, to follow them. To our present-day experience, they already begin to manifest an other-worldly majesty.

Even if in modern composition these elements are used primarily as a means to express irony, provocation and the like, still they herald the shifts we have spoken of clearly enough.

What we have said should be sufficient stimulus for the reader to take note of the relation of the school of singing here discussed to contemporary questions in music. One may listen to the latest creations of our contemporary musicians and read what they have to say.

Rudolf Steiner spoke in no uncertain terms about a major turning point in the middle of this century, and about its background in terms of the history of evolution.

11

We would like to go into just one of his statements, because it throws a special light on the aims of this school. In one of his lectures on social questions, given in 1918, Rudolf Steiner characterised in a broad context the respective missions of the different cultural areas. The peoples of the West he described as tending primarily towards technical tasks, those of the East as particularly gifted in relation to eugenics (to be sure, in a higher sense than this concept is usually accorded today); but the peoples of the Centre, he said, are disposed in the depths of their being towards developing therapeutic forces. In this connection the following statement holds true: the people of this middle region will realise the full magnitude of their therapeutic mission only when they have thoroughly understood — and this means through all the powers of scientific research as well — that the course of human life is really identical with that of a disease. Then they will strive to bring the appropriate healing forces to man at each stage of his development, in order to counterbalance the symptoms of decay as life progresses. Education, for example, would become a matter of therapy; healing would permeate it down to the smallest details. Viewed in this way, the whole domain of the arts also falls under a new light.

This idea should not really seem strange to us: the art of all great cultures of earlier times was naturally imbued with an inherent therapeutic quality.

In face of the obvious rapid decline of our culture (Albert Schweizer compared it to a boat torn by a raging current towards a cataract), it would be expected that these insights should break through and call forth profound changes in attitude. We can envisage, and hope for, a cultural stream which would set the development of therapeutic forces at the heart of human life; for in such a setting, this school could demonstrate its mission. Thus it seems significant that, as destiny would have it, in the decades after this book was published the author devoted her attention almost entirely to the therapeutic possibilities of this school of singing. With the collaboration of doctors such as Dr. Eugen Kolisko, the first school physician in the pedagogical movement of the free Waldorf Schools, and also through the help and interest of Dr. Karl König, known for his world-wide work in curative education, a wealth of experience has been gathered in the field of curative singing. However, there can be no thought of making this public until this school of singing has met with wider recognition.

How is it possible that something of such significance should be so little known to the public? One answer among many to this question woud run as follows: we have had to bow before the fact that changes long overdue in this century have been mightily hindered by retarding powers.

Up till now, the genuine innovations of our time have been confined almost exclusively to the realm of technical achievement. To any person of insight, it is clear that an inner aspect must counterbalance this outward orientation if we are to avoid serious social disorders. However, our cultural life, which might promote these inner forces, has come under a disturbing dependency on economic and governmental functioning. Despite the catastrophes that have twice shaken the world to its foundations, social forms have sunk back into their former state again and again. In these circumstances, what contemporary spiritual life by rights should be has hardly been able to unfold at all, or only in a distorted way. Still, in the long run nothing will be able to hinder the needed changes from breaking through, save complete destruction of Western culture. We stand before a difficult choice indeed. At present we see genuine and justified strivings asserting themselves — for example, in the student movements; but they are very much distorted by obstructive forces. The youth is calling urgently for the true face of the age, for the rightful cultural and spiritual situation of our times. But the wars have destroyed so much which might already have nurtured and which we bitterly miss today. Many of the most able fell in battle; only a few still carry with them the sense and tasks of our century uncompromisingly into the future.

The new beginnings in all areas of cultural life which have sprung from Rudolf Steiner's spiritual science were founded with an eye for the future. In face of the devastations of our times, only the very smallest part of these cultural seeds has been able to sprout and unfold into visible blossoming.

This work represents one such seed, scarcely past the first stages of germination — a seed for the true fructification of our culture and of our life together.

It seems to us more than coincidence that the one who opened up this path was a member of the Swedish people. The language of Scandinavia is so inclined to song and has been home to so many outstanding singers; furthermore, the untamed elemental power of the land can impart to the receptive among its children a rich dowry of ancient instinctive nature-wisdom.

The author, still active at the advanced age of 90 with unbroken vigour in mind and body, looks towards the coming generations with the hope that there will be devoted and gifted people among them to foster this life's work, achieved with untiring effort, and develop it for the benefit of many.

The reader may have gathered that this is not just another book on voice training. It is not written primarily for the sake of amateur singers, nor for the aesthete who uses art to escape for a while from the harrassment and stress of life; rather, it intends a new attitude: an earnest sense of responsibility towards our time and the people moulding their destiny within it in all places and conditions. Here, this attitude expresses itself in the call to work for the purity and preservation of true singing.

St. John's Day, 1969 Jürgen Schriefer

TO LOUIS MICHAEL JULIUS WERBECK

*To you my most beloved life-companion, I
dedicate this book. Although you have
long since stepped across the boundary
into the spiritual world, still the bond
between us, which nourished this work
from the beginning, has continued to
guide it to its final end.*

Riesengebirge, Bohemia 1935-36

FOREWORD

When one wishes to report on something altogether new in book-form — something that has been lifted out of the very element of life — one must find new concepts and coin new names before one can attempt to present it. This can only be achieved by holding to the organic process through which it has itself come into being. For this reason I have tried to describe this school of singing objectively, as it matures through its own inherent power into a self-contained organism.

However, if one wishes to gain a deeper understanding for the way in which such a new living entity arises, one must direct a certain interest towards its 'birth', insofar as it comes into being at a definite moment. This makes one aware that lawful patterns are at work not only in the growth of a living thing, but that the 'birth' itself also crystallises out of the greater organic context.

This, however, means that we must look at the human individuality as a whole — at how it fits, with its personal destiny, into the stream of events, and how the personal interacts with the objective. Then we can see that this birth into the world is likewise determined by an organic process of becoming.

Thus, although the personal should usually remain in the background, in this case I have no choice but to set about my task on a purely personal basis: with a short description of my own path of development in the field of singing.

So the reader may excuse it if I try quite simply to show

how I arrived at the way of singing in the most natural way, directly out of my almost childishly naive life; and I will describe it just as it comes naturally to me.

I was born in the far North of Sweden. For as far as my memory reaches back, my childhood flowed in the most intimate contact with nature. From early morning till dark I would roam tirelessly in the woods and meadows – mostly alone, always singing, a sandwich in my pocket. Picking flowers was my highest joy; for an especially beautiful one I risked my young life more than once. Or I flew about on the sledge run or the skating ring, and also sped through the world ice-skate-sailing or on skis. Thus I was a 'wild young one' and defended my freedom with fierce tenacity. As they say, I was 'no easy child'; but my loving parents, who were both extremely musical, never tried to break this energy of mine with force. And it is no doubt this fact that I must thank for the strength I have preserved for later life and its tasks.

Singing, as I said, was something I had always been able to do. In fact, I was probably something of a child prodigy; but this troubled me very little. For one thing, no one tried to tame the wild creature that I was; and for another, the life of a 'wunderkind' in the country is completely different from that in the city. I only know that I was particularly fond of going around to the houses of family friends as a 'travelling singer'. I would appear there in the twilight hours with my guitar, which I had learned to play without help, and would play the old, mostly very sentimental, soulful folk-ballads and songs until my listeners showed tears – at which point I would go my way 'satisfied'. . . .

When I came to school, my solo-singing along with the choir was such a natural thing that I was not in the least surprised to be taken to a public church concert; (the profit was to go for a new organ). I did become a bit doubtful, though, when I had a closer look at the 'grand soloist' of the evening. She was an opera singer; and since the top notes were difficult for her, she – quite understandably – made strange movements with her head, something like a rooster getting ready to crow. This made the audience laugh a little.... I, however, was determined never to become a 'grand soloist'.

Singing was simply my element. I did not know any 'difficulties' at all – neither in the highest registers (remarkably, the three-line G# and A [G#''' and A''']) came quite easily to me), nor in the low ones. Breathing troubles – they did not exist. The coloratura (except the trill, which I first learned in the conservatory) came of its own accord; and as for my performing ability – it was hardly to be complained of. This was because of the natural humour and the urge to imitate which had probably stayed with me from my earliest childhood.

I simply could not grasp how people could become 'hoarse' or 'tired' from singing (as I gathered from the talk of grown-ups) – for me it was just the most direct expression of my whole, untroubled child's being.

Before long, however, I was to learn painfully enough that there can be real low points on the road to singing. At the age of fifteen, I entered the Royal Academy of Music in Stockholm as a singing pupil. Although I had a very kind and careful teacher, who lovingly went along with my own particular manner, still I slowly began to feel ill-at-ease when singing the customary exercises: I *noticed* – that I was singing. Until then, the *activity* of singing had remained completely unconscious for me. This feeling grew more and more intense in the course of the instruction, and finally I noticed that at unguarded moments I was beginning to sing with very awkward mouth positions.

Naturally I had also been infected with the generally

prevalent desire to have a 'big', that is, a 'strong' voice; for, though my voice was very endurant, it could really not have been called 'big' – quite the contrary! Measured against the voices of my fellow pupils, it was quite plainly small. Thus, a voluntary desire to strengthen my voice came very much to the fore. This, of course, only increased the objective feeling of discomfort in me, which clearly pointed to an organic change within my singing instrument.

After I had been studying with her for about two and a half years, my teacher fell ill, and I was to be given another teacher, a man. But this teacher's way of singing was so shocking to me that, in order to escape the dreaded lessons, in my child's helplessness I simulated illness. In fact, this illness was not so utterly without grounds; for though I still could sing, a very strange affection of the neck glands slowly arose. The doctors could not understand its origin, but it gradually began to impair my singing in a clearly audible way.

By special permission, I even made concert tours on my own during this time; and outwardly they were successful. For my part, however, I was slowly losing my joy in singing. The troubles grew, the highest tones of the three line octave began to be lost; and as for the coloratura, which had come quite naturally earlier, I had to practise it systematically to be able to make use of it – in short, all the signs of an impending collapse slowly set in. Nevertheless I endured the course of instruction for two further years, and in the meantime entered the opera school affiliated with the musical academy, in order to prepare for my debut on the Court stage. Then, in my twenty-first year, I made my debut as 'Mignon', 'Susanne' (The Marriage of Figaro), and 'Lakmé', whereupon I was immediately accepted as a member of the Court Opera.

Now my voice was placed under very great demands

20

indeed. Despite the slow 'decline' just mentioned, I was still able to meet these demands, although only through great exertions. In a single season, for example, I studied and sang eight large leading roles. But... at the price of much sacrifices and drastic cures! I would have to write a long time to describe them all. Because of their tragi-comic nature, let me select just one of these. In the country at that time, most floors were of planed but unpainted wood, and people scrubbed them on their hands and knees. Each morning of a performance found me in this position scouring and rinsing with all my strength, until after about an hour of work, sometimes still longer, I had warmed myself through sufficiently; then the hoarse veils which almost always covered my voice had been 'washed away', and it was 'free' for the performance.

In the midst of this martyrdom, of which the uninitiated suspected nothing, a beneficial stagnation set in when the Academy allotted me a fairly large travelling stipend for further study abroad. That was a great relief for me!

In Paris, in Italy, in Germany I searched for a new, wholesome kind of singing; but everywhere in vain....

However, while I was in Munich at the end of this period of study, negotiations were being conducted for a guest performance at the opera there. For various reasons this guest performance did not take place; but this circumstance brought me into personal acquaintance with the opera's then highly celebrated tenor, Heinrich Knote. He was not only a famous singer, but also had a very good reputation as a singing teacher. One day, when we had sung through the bridal chamber scene from 'Lohengrin' together, and were exchanging our views on the field of singing pedagogy, in his objective enthusiasm for the art he came out with the following words: 'You have,' he said, 'in your heart, in your throat and in your understanding, absolutely everything you could wish for; but with the school by which you are singing, you will be able to continue only two years at the most. There was one tone that you sang quite differently from all the others; why don't you sing all tones so — through the nose?' I listened closely and sang the note (it was F''); and I had to admit that it sounded different from all the others. But a certain dullness had spread over my hearing as well, so that I was unable to bring this difference to full consciousness. Remarkably, I did not at first attribute any special importance to this meeting; in fact I had actually forgotten his words very soon.

Then, when I was back in my homeland again and had just completed my twenty-fifth year of life (I was still singing the first parts with the Court Opera), I contracted a sort of paralysis of the vocal cords. In any case my voice simply refused to work! I was actually not surprised, for the outcome could not have been very different. Now I knew clearly enough that I had nothing more to lose, and everything to gain; and above all, I knew from the negative experience of my study trips that I could only save myself *out of my own resources.*

In this grave moment of inner and outer helplessness, remembrance of the days in Munich and of Heinrich Knote's words re-emerged in me like a kind gift. How quickly his prediction had come true!

Now, since I could not sing the tones any longer, I began to direct *the sound through my nose while speaking.* However, since this was also extremely difficult in the first stage of the collapse, I tried to *listen for* the *silent* tones, to bring them into reality in my hearing. And now I became aware that those words: 'Why don't you sing through the nose?', had been branded into my soul without my knowing it; for now all my striving was aimed just at this. I spoke nasally and tried to hold the speaking sound, to draw it out until it became a half-sung tone. On this tone I concentrated all the power of my attention.

Upon this, the memory of my voice as a child emerged again in an incredibly vivid way!

The silvery ring that had been in my tones came before me almost as an independent entity, and prompted me to look for the speech sound that would best let it come through.... And so I found the sound — NG! This was a very meaningful discovery for me! I actually knew right away that this was the only place to seek a new beginning; and the success of this 'exercise' also seemed almost a miracle. In the space of just a few weeks I had got my voice back again, and since the breakdown had happened at the beginning of my summer vacation, I was able to take up my public activity anew with the beginning of the season. Now, however, singing became practically torture for me. It was a continual matter of compromising between the new and the old ways of singing. The latter naturally tried to assert itself strongly, while the new way was so tender, so completely different, that I felt as though I were between two worlds at war with one another.

As my marriage brought me to Germany, which had always been the 'land of my dream', my connection with the Court Opera ended. A period of highly concentrated concert and guest performances followed, taking me to almost every country in Europe. I was able to meet these demands only by practising according to my new school between performances, and especially in the vacations. In this way the damage was repeatedly healed and forestalled by the new way of singing.

Still, although there was no lack of recognition, distinctions and other 'honours' — which are simply inseparable from such a career — this life became more and more unbearable for me. At the height of my career as an artist, I had only one longing: to 'make an end', to put my new school on firm foundations and build it up. During the war I made many more trips, and it was not until the very beginning of the post-war period, when the world situation brought hardships of many kinds, that I took this — along with my growing distaste for public activity — as an excuse to withdraw. Several other things as well, among them the death of my husband, played a great part in this decision. Now I was free to build up my school.

* * * * *

I would like now to show how I came to regard this task as a truly *great* and *important* one. Naturally, so long as all my powers were absorbed in my own voice troubles, the thought never occurred to me that my struggles to restore my singing instrument could be of significance for any other human being — the more so since I could not see clearly whether what I was attempting was really right in the end. In that time of slight doubt, something occurred that for me bore the character of a special event — something that was to prove of eminent importance for my work and for me: through a personal interview, I came to know Rudolf Steiner. The reason I had sought him out had nothing immediately to do with my problems and questions in singing. So I was all the more amazed when Rudolf Steiner came up to me with his open cordiality, and spontaneously said a few words. Although they appear to be of a quite personal nature, and thus could be easily misunderstood, I wish to put them down here, because in the context of this book they take on a meaning that must be seen as objective. And so, to my greatest surprise, at that moment Rudolf Steiner said to me: 'What a beautiful etheric larynx you have! I do not want to be immodest, but it seems to me that you sing as I speak. And isn't it true, if one did not speak or sing with sublimated air –, the throat might not be equal to the demands placed on it?' By this he apparently meant both his own activity as a public speaker as well as my copious singing.

This appears, as I said, to be a quite personal and perhaps not at all so significant episode; but anyone who has come to know the personality of Rudolf Steiner, knows that things he said often as though in passing were of greater significance than would usually be the case. One may take this as one will, but for me these words gave nourishment over a long period of time. This confirmation that I was doing the right thing, expressed in such an unusual description of the element of air (one that I could never have invented at that time), and the parallel drawn between speaking and singing, gave me the first inkling that my work might also be of fundamental importance.

Encouraged by these thoughts, I applied all my powers to achieve results in such a way that I could also speak about them, i.e. ask questions.

And so the situation changed for me entirely. When concrete questions and difficulties came up which I could not solve, I was able to go to Rudolf Steiner for advice — no doubt every time with a pounding heart. And I must admit that each time I felt like a very insignificant little beginner; for to my great amazement I had to realise that the problems I was wrestling with were already well known to him out of his work; and sometimes he unravelled a tangled knot with a single sentence. So it went with many of my questions. But there was more than this: he set me tasks and confirmed what I had discovered myself in between meetings. It even happened that he designed an exercise to improve an organic articulatory defect in one of my pupils;

25

and it did always achieve a very positive effect after some time. In short, for me it was a completely new way of working!

In the meantime, a school had arisen out of those beginnings. I was approached and asked to give an oral explanation of the principles of this singing school.

In view of the relationship to Rudolf Steiner which had developed for my work, I saw it as necessary to ask for his agreement at this turning point. And thereupon, he gave what was for me an extraordinarily interesting and significant summary of his view of the school. In its essential content, here is what he said: This school will be individually very different in its stages and phases of development. The 'what' of the school is naturally the same for everyone, but the 'how' — the way each one will experience it — is dependent on the individual gifts and constitution of the student. It is not at all necessary that all students have the same experiences as I have. The essential thing with such experiences is ultimately only the capacity to be sensitive to the delicate transitional moments between two different stages. Such capacities are not seldom determined by a particular folk or cultural background.

In this connection, Rudolf Steiner said that the folk background and mother tongue out of which a person has formed his singing organisation was of tremendous importance. Particularly favourable languages are Italian and Swedish, because they have more rounded sound forms. In this way they have a most favourable action on the child's organisation; and so (these were his words) it is already a particular gift of destiny to be born a singer in Sweden. In this, Rudolf Steiner saw my personal part in this work and school.

If one takes this fully into consideration, then it is possible to speak of this school as having an objectively spiritual-scientific content at its base.

To my great joy, Rudolf Steiner told me then that I might put forth this school of singing as sanctioned by him and established on the basis of spiritual science. And this did take place later.

I then gave public courses and lectures about the school. In addition I composed the first sketch for this book, though it was not until after Rudolf Steiner's death that I first wrote it down. At that time my life's companion, Louis Werbeck, still stood by my side supportively, ready to help. Together we worked out the first chapter, which appeared in somewhat changed form as an essay in the magazine *Die Individualität* then newly founded. Since then, around ten years have passed, during which I have not been able to find the opportunity and leisure to continue the work. There was enough to do by way of organising and building up the school. Pupils had to be taught; and beyond this, as things developed, various areas of application appeared for this kind of singing. Among other things there was a lively collaboration with various physicians who were extremely interested in its therapeutic effects.

Here I would like to take the opportunity to express my heartfelt thanks to a personality very closely bound up with this side of my work, Dr. Eugen Kolisko, for the constant, warm, and unselfish interest with which he stood by me through this whole time, helping, counselling and protecting. Dr. Kolisko first tried to enter into the life of the school himself, and in this way he created the basis for a real, earnest collaboration in the field of singing *therapy*.

Later on, lectures were given by Dr. Kolisko on the therapeutic aspect of this way of singing, for which illustrative examples were provided by the school's choir and by me. This first occurred in 1928 in London and in 1929 in Hamburg. In May of 1933, Dr. Kolisko gave a lengthy lecture cycle for a number of students on the nature of singing and its therapeutic effects (*Das Wesen des Singens und seine therapeutischen Wirkungen*). Most particularly, however, I am thankful to him for his contribution to this book; for although this whole work is oriented chiefly towards the artistic experience and acquisition of true singing, the living picture of this school — the essential aim for which it strives — can only be seen completely by considering both its spiritual-scientific foundations as well as its prospects for therapeutic application. For this reason I am very glad and thankful for his Afterword.

Likewise, I feel impelled at this point to recall another personality with cordial thanks, Miss W. Roelvink. Through her never-slackening interest and tireless work for this school and its growth, standing next to me in true friendship, she took many a burden off my shoulders.

Now I would like to bring these personal considerations to an end in order to pass on to the actual content of this book. I set a few words of Goethe as a motto at the beginning.

MOTTO:

... Dich im Unendlichen zu finden,
musst unterscheiden und dann verbinden;...

(To find yourself in the infinite,
you must distinguish and then unite;)

(from *Atmosphäre* by Goethe)

Chapter One

INTRODUCTION

When Goethe contemplated the world of plants, before his inner eye he saw the 'Urpflanze', the archetypal plant — creator of all that sprouts and blooms. It was given to him to perceive the real being which stands behind and originates the world we see spread out in front of us as the green plant-cover of the earth. For this reason he was able, like no other, to grasp the spatial, visible phenomena of the plant world.

In investigating the secrets of the plant world, Goethe first gathered experience after experience through observation of single typical facts; these he felt through and illuminated with his artist's phantasy, until they revealed to him what they had in common, so that the being producing the phenomena, the 'idea' of the 'Urpflanze', could be born in his soul. We must search today in the same way if we wish to learn about the secrets of the essential active principle which must exist behind the manifestations of the human voice.

As Goethe observed the individual plants in order to grasp that which was common to them, so we must let the manifestations of the world of tone work upon us in order to find what they possess in common. Our ear must learn to listen inwardly, expectantly to them, until they uncover for us the principle common to them all: in our soul, the idea of the archetypal human voice must light up — the archetypal sound underlying all the manifoldness of the

30

tonal world. (See translator's note.) Just as the 'Urpflanze' stays hidden behind the sensible forms in which it manifests itself, so the archetypal voice remains hidden from outward perception. And just as the 'Urpflanze' is the entity which creates all apparent phenomena in the plant world, so the archetypal voice — or better, the archetypal sound — is the creative ground of all human vocal manifestation.

This comparison may seem bold or strange; yet taking into account the basic difference between natural and human creation, it is fully justified: just as the various species of plant arise through the meeting of the plant archetype with the earth, in the same way human vocal manifestations come about through the meeting of the archetypal sound with its earthly vehicles — human physical organisations.

The Goethean 'Urpflanze' is spiritually 'visible', but not audible; the archetypal sound, however, can be not only grasped, but also heard in the sphere of the ideal. Goethe's 'Urpflanze' becomes visible in the ideal world.* The archetypal sound becomes ideally visible and audible, for it is more than a picture: it manifests itself simultaneously as idea *and* sound.

When we learn to give ourselves over to the guidance of our inner and outer ear — the 'expectant listening' mentioned above, listening for the hidden sound — then this tone-originating principle will become inwardly audible to us, and in our own tones this archetypal sound will also slowly begin to glow through in their outer resonance. Thus, as it becomes more and more apparent to the outer ear, it will gradually unveil and free itself from the tones which are bound by the physical body.

*It becomes visible through what he calls the 'anschauende Urteils-kraft' — the power to penetrate to the inner nature of a phenomenon through direct perception.

Paul Bruns, a recently deceased singing teacher and author who on many points came very close to the true secrets of a genuine art and pedagogy of singing, speaks of this fundamental fact (although he certainly did not recognise it in its true character). In his book *Das Problem der Kontra-Altstimme* (The Problem of the Contralto Voice) p. 44, he says: 'Hearing becomes an art. The purely sensory, outer perception must be complemented by the spiritual perception of the inner ear, if one wishes to really grasp what is essential in vocal sound.'

All work, all efforts towards what is called voice-training — basically it is nothing other than a freeing, a clearing away of the obstructive coverings which will not let the voice 'come out' (as the current expression quite rightly puts it).

And here we encounter the cardinal error of today's singing pedagogy: the human 'voice' needs no 'training' — it is already there, finished and perfect as an entity sounding in the ideal world. What it is waiting for is — *liberation*! We should speak of freeing the voice, or better yet *uncovering the voice*, and not *voice-training*.

One who has not tried to penetrate into the actual experience of the art of singing might take this statement as a sort of empty phrase. However, for the one who honestly devotes himself to objective study and comes to his own knowledge through experience, this sentence signifies nothing less than the key to real singing — that is, to the kind of singing *appropriate for the present and near future*.

At this point, our comparison between the Goethean approach to natural-scientific research and the exploration of the mysteries of the human voice must be extended to the level of method; for the progress of science from mechanical to organic conceptions rests on Goethe's ability not only to observe exactly (which the mechanists have also brought to a masterful level), but especially to penetrate intuitively, empirically into the world of the Ideal, the Original. As this second gift of Goethe's has dwindled among men of today, the science of materialism has created the greatness of our age in technological culture, on the one hand; but on the other, it has also brought about its inner misery by estranging human beings from the world of spirit and soul. The spirit of natural science has penetrated and transformed all areas of life, expanding them without limit materially, but at the same time impoverishing them of content; it also has penetrated into the spiritual sciences, the humanities — at first unconsciously, unnoticed by its bearers, and therefore uncontested.

In this way it also penetrated into teaching of all kinds, and thus into the teaching of singing as well. And although artistic education defied its opponent long enough, through the heightened feeling for life among its teachers, still, it too fell before this monstrous, all-levelling spirit in the end.

In one way or another, the singing methods which are found under a hundred different names nowadays (methods that pull the practice of artistic singing down to the sphere of more or less mechanistic, over-sophisticated exercises) are influenced and determined by the spirit of natural science. The uncontested authority of natural science has been victorious here as well; and no one can brighten the chaos that reigns in the field of singing teaching — as in hardly any other field of culture — who is not ready to go right to the root of the evil. What must be done is to replace the surface-knowledge with a fundamental knowledge, i.e., to penetrate from an outside to an inside view of singing.

To speak of archetypal phenomena — or even of *the* archetypal phenomenon — in the tone realm in a similar manner to the way in which Goethe spoke of the archetypal phenomena or phenomenon in the plant realm — this alone can bring us a decisive step forward. Only that which has been studied and raised to scientific knowledge in this way will meet the requirements that are rooted deeply in evolutionary necessities of our times. All else — both the little reforms of that which the materialistic demon has brought about, as well as all relapses into what existed in the past — is nothing but a side-track in development, and must ultimately lead to a dead end.

In the art of singing and in its teaching — as in every other field — a new start from the very beginning is needed; i.e., we must look for the essential starting point which is capable of leading us to a right posing of the question, and thus to the prospect of a satisfying answer. However, in our times any truly new beginning requires us to go back consciously to the fundamentals; and we must go back not by means of theoretically-tinged conceptions, but through a direct living and doing, by way of a real know-how. In short, it must be through a doing in reality, which cannot be replaced by any scientific sense — no matter how well educated, nor by any scientific training — no matter how thorough.

One basic origin of the misery prevailing in today's teaching and art of singing lies simply in the false conception we have formed of the human voice, a conception which has arisen out of the spirit of materialism. We think of the voice, by analogy to the physical world, as an extremely sublimated 'material' (it is no accident that we speak of 'voice-material'); and we try to form this 'material' in the way that something material, inorganic, can be moulded: mechanically and from the outside.

Thought is always behind critical choices or new beginnings (at least, this is so in our time), and determines whether they will lead in a wholesome or a harmful direction.

34

Thinking asks: What makes the tone? Materialistic thinking answers: Matter. From its standpoint this is the only possible answer, and thus an unshakeable one.

However, if the tone is of material organic origin, then it can only be of a material nature itself; and if the tone is of a material nature, then it is quite rightly treated as matter, and the product is — chaos.

The 'voice' is manipulated as a thing in a variety of materially-conceived ways: we 'give it a foundation', 'push' it, 'hold' it, and divide it mechanically into different registers, etc. It has become a thing; one does not try to set it free and reveal it, but simply to form and mould it from without.

As a teacher and an artist, however, one can never do anything but create the conditions under which the phenomenon of the voice — by its nature immaterial — might manifest itself.

Most immediately involved in providing these conditions are, of course, the ear, larynx, and respiratory organs, as well as, for the textual element, our whole speech organisation (tongue, lips, jaws, palate, etc.) In actuality, as we shall see later, it is the entire human organism that sounds. In fact, the *whole human body* is particularly disposed for correct singing. It could simply be called an *extended larynx;* and the work that must be accomplished for the uncovering of the voice can be characterised thus: To the extent that one succeeds in making one's bodily instrument open for the sound to penetrate and shine through, to that extent the tone will appear beautiful or not beautiful. It will sound beautiful when nothing of the bodily nature hinders it in flowing through. It will sound badly when it is 'held' or 'caught' as it streams through. Once one has recognised this primary fact about the 'voice', then one knows what is essential: the voice manifests itself out of the inaudible realm. With this knowledge, the materialistic orientation is simply reversed: it is not the material-organic level that produces the tone; rather, the inaudible voice produces it on the basis of the material-organic level.

When one has learned this truth through one's own experience, an understanding of the therapeutic action of correct singing naturally follows. It becomes clear that the voice as such can never fall ill, but that healing forces must be inherent in it. Just as it is a mistake, from the standpoint of true knowledge, to speak of a disease of the spirit, so it is also a mistake to speak of a disease of the voice.

If the fundamental view of today's singing teaching — that the physical organisation of man produces the tone — is a false one, what is it then (this question now *must* be posed) that sounds, that makes tones?

The answer will not come to us out of the conventional science. For it mistakenly believes that the sensible tone is the result of the oscillating body (of course there is no dispute that it oscillates). In order to understand that the tone-originating principle, the sound-mediating instrument, cannot be found within the material nature of the organism, it is only necessary to recall certain facts: All states of oscillation in a physical body can be traced back to a cause. In the case of a chiming bell, for instance, these causes can be found on the outside; not so in the case of human vocal manifestations. An invisible inner impulse, not to be compared with outward causation, makes it so that we discover *effects* in the physical organism which cannot be there through themselves. The causation can be sought and found only in a principle within the human being. Outward science has no access to this causative principle, due to the peculiarity of its means of investigation. If we wish to get beyond the mere recognition of these effects and reveal the causes in their actuality, we must apply methods of research

36

capable of comprehending this insensible, inner-human principle. These methods do exist in spiritual science. It knows of the original tone-producing instrument of our organism — it is the so-called etheric body or formative-force body — and can give most extensive information about it.* Thus, one can now feel that henceforth no teaching and art of singing can be appropriate for our times without a science capable of penetrating into its inner realm.

Older epochs of art did not require explanation; they could do without such a scientific foundation. Today this has necessarily become different. More and more people in these generations will be in a position to sense the existence of this incorporeal instrument which sounds in itself; and then they will know out of their own experience that it cannot be identified with the physical body.

Even at the beginning of their discoveries, such people will clearly sense this sounding entity and notice that it projects beyond the physical body in all directions. Later, when their experience begins to differentiate itself, they will be aware of a certain sound-centre above their head, and will also know this sounding organisation beneath their feet. In this way they will *experience* that this sounding principle is not the same as the limited, physical, three-dimensional body. Out of personal experience gained independently of spiritual science, they will have to confirm what spiritual investigation tells us.

*See G. Wachsmuth's 'Etheric Formative Forces in Cosmos, Earth and Man' (London 1932), as well as Dr. H. Poppelbaum's book 'Der Bilde-kräfteleib der Lebewesen als Gegenstand wissenschaftlicher Erfahrung' (Stuttgart 1924), and his article 'The Etheric in Idea and Action' from the Medical Yearbook of the Goetheanum, Vol. III, translated by George Adams.

In truth there are many such human beings today. They are unconsciously looking for spiritual science, and in the meantime torment themselves with the unsolved riddles.

Thus it may be stated, both out of experience and in accordance with spiritual science: *The etheric body streams through the physical body and sounds out into the world and cosmos, when it is not held back and hindered in its sound-unfolding by the physical body.* Human beings of all times have known very well of this connection of their sensible manifestation of sound with its supersensible manifestation in the cosmos. They experienced this cosmic relation of the tone which flowed through them, and therefore felt reverence and awe before the art of song. We have lost this consciousness: we believe that our material organism itself produces the tones as states of vibration in the air! Tones, to physics, are nothing (they are the measurable states of vibration of sensibly tangible elements). Through this view we have lost any kind of devotion and reverence towards the art of singing. What has remained for us is the outer aesthetic pleasure, the egoism of enjoyment in the sensation of sound.

To be sure, we have not forgotten this of our own will. We have necessarily forgotten what constituted the inner bliss of former times and the otherworldliness of most ancient times, because we live in a time of materialism, a time of a real domination of matter over soul and spirit. Therefore we have been given physical organs which are hardened, inflexible, and impenetrable. Our physical larynx, taken as a whole instrument, has become 'wooden', and our speech organisation has hardened. Compared to older times, both of our singing organisations are much more unwieldy, inflexible, impermeable, and thus less suitable for the art of singing.

This fundamental realisation illuminates a number of

38

things for us which otherwise would remain not under-standable: the fact, for example, that the vocal range of singers is shrinking more and more; today we have few high sopranos and tenors, and also few low altos and basses.

To say that an organ becomes hard, 'wooden', is the same as to say it becomes unelastic. However, if the larynx becomes unelastic, then it is *self-understood* that the singer loses tones at the upper and lower limits first, because they call for the greatest finesse in regard to attack and tension of the organs. Thus, the middle range develops at the expense of the high and low tones.

That things were once different can be gathered from the compositions of masters who lived even in the last two centuries, particularly those of the old Italians. We see that these musicians — who, after all, composed for their con-temporary singers — gave not only the sopranos and tenors difficult coloraturas to sing, but also the alto and bass voices: a sign that the constitution of the larynx was not yet so hardened, which permitted the artists to connect them-selves with the tones more easily than is possible today.

A further indication can be seen in the fact that it was not customary to compose with a strict distinction between soprano and alto parts. In previous centuries it was rather the timbre than the range of the voices which determined the assignment of the various roles. Voices were simply not so reduced in range; whoever had a voice had all the tones at his disposal (the contralto had the full soprano range, the soprano could sing the contralto's low notes), but naturally also had one region within the whole scale in which he felt especially well and at home. This region, whether high or low, had an immediate relation to the individual timbre of his voice.

Now, however, we have gone so far on the road of decadence that we even begin to lose the tones themselves:

on average we still possess only half of the old voice range.

And the decline goes rapidly onward. This elementary fact naturally forces itself on all who are active as teachers in the field of voice or singing in our times. It becomes a problem for them all; and they try to solve it in reference to the organ which appears to produce the tone — the physical larynx and the organs associated with it. However, they will never find the solution to the riddle if they continue to investigate and work in this direction; for, even if they speak of the opposite, they are searching along the road of the mechanical and dead instead of the organic, the living, and the soul-spiritual.

Our reference to the reduction in range of the human voice, which arises through the progressive hardening of the organs, points to only one of the problems with which the present times are struggling. However, without the help of genuine spiritual investigation it will be impossible to solve them all.

To conduct research and exploration out of the art itself — as we in fact intend here — for this, spiritual science was not really necessary. It only confirmed the results found in the independent field of singing. Just as Goethe came to the experience of the 'Urpflanze' without spiritual science, in the same way the research results reported here were found independently, without recourse to spiritual science. However, to understand the experiences that came in the course if the research, and to understand them in a way appropriate to the nature of our times — for this spiritual science was needed. Thus, it would not be enough for these times just to hear of the 'idea' of the archetypal voice. Our times no longer have any right relation to intuitions and their realities. If, however, this 'idea' is confirmed afterwards by supersensible research, through an exact science of the spirit, then it can be understood and accepted in a new way by the scientific consciousness of our age.

When the teacher and artist has turned towards research in the direction of the inner and spiritual, he enters on a path of slow and laborious wandering. He is approaching experiences that will shake him, bring him pain, doubt, happiness – in short, everything that stirs a person most deeply in his soul. In truth, he will not come easily to what must be called the research-results of his particular work.

These experiences are of such a kind as to be *extraordinarily* difficult to describe. Something that manifests itself only in the fluid element of life itself, and only for fleeting moments – to clothe this in words, to put it in new conceptual vessels: this is a hard task. Coming as they do on the background of intensive work and a given talent, these experiences are surely easier to come to than to describe in such a way that they can be fruitful for someone who wishes to use them for orientation on his own path of study.

For this reason, without a high degree of trust and a truly good will, one will necessarily misunderstand the following presentation of our findings.

A school that wishes to provide genuinely new experiences and discoveries cannot really be 'accepted' in the trivial sense of the word. The representatives of the old schools will even *have to* reject it, due to their particular conceptions. And the singer who feels himself indebted to the old schools for his art will be able to experience the content of the new school only with enormous difficulty, because of his mis-education. Then again, those who have as yet had no training will take it quite without criticism, or at best without prejudice. They can be convinced only through the gradual appearance of results and moments of metamorphosis. In short, a new school of singing has every chance of being misunderstood, especially when it has to seek its epistemological foundation in a science of the spirit, not in a science which is current and accepted.

Two unconditional requirements must be fulfilled before we can achieve anything. First, we must learn to seek only in the actual doing; and in the process we must explore with the utmost attentiveness of the ear. We must be able to be there with all of our power, all of our love; we must be actively engaged while concentrating our powers on one point without tiring. For it is an inexorable law, and applies to this research as well: only to the extent that we push our powers beyond the limit of comfort do we transform ourselves; and only through steady transformation do we progress. The second requirement is that, besides devoting all of our active powers to the work, we consciously strive to acquire the gift of objective observation for whatever wishes to 'reveal' itself, independently of our will.

When we have developed this new gift of observation, when the first new phenomena come into our field of consciousness, then what has been observed must be retained with the subtle inner organs, then this new thing must, above all, be protected from adulteration with products of thought or phantasy. For it will be belittled, distorted, falsified and trivialised by secret opponents of progress; but if one keeps the phenomenon pure from all admixture and seeks to evoke it repeatedly, then it will consolidate into a conclusive fact. Only after one can deal with this new reality as a practical exercise does one have the right to attempt a verbal formulation of it. Whoever understands what is meant here knows that especially with a new attainment, it is not good to subject it to thought too early.

Once the new attainment has become a possession of our

understanding, then we can speak about it with unerring certainty and calm. And when one speaks about something, of which one knows that its original ground is in a higher sphere of reality, one is prompted inwardly to speak about this higher reality in a different way than one might speak about a commonly accepted reality.

The words 'reveal itself' were chosen above with due consideration. The artist and investigator who begins to recognise and employ this principle of 'revelation' in the depths and earnestness of his being, comes to feel an ever-growing modesty and humility when he turns to his responsible work: 'As a self-seeking and wilful human being I am only a hindrance, a nothing, in the face of that which wills to manifest itself; I must acquire a completely new sensibility, a new orientation, if I am to be worthy of a revelation.' He will have such feelings, and will recognise that without educating himself in the right way, he will never reach his goal.

Such experiences, touching the human being *as a whole*, tend of themselves to form his whole view of life. It would be right to say: scientific seriousness is joined by a religious feeling. A person senses: this path of exploration is at once artistic, religious, and scientific. Therefore it can be understood that the results won on such a path not only have an artistically-obligating character, but also engage the moral life of the human being.

To be allowed to be a servant of art, to will to serve the whole of art and not one's personal well being — such is the result and fruit of this particular path of research.

For truly, whoever will climb up to that higher reality must step through a narrow portal, the portal of a new kind of artistic sensibility. Whoever wishes to pass through this portal in order to conduct research out of egoistic motives, he will be struck blind and deaf, as it were. He will

43

find phantoms and errors, and present them to the world. The condition for finding the real and true is: to wait in humility and unshakeable perseverance for those hours in which the deeper mysteries of the soul desire to reveal themselves.

Then one day, during intensive practice, something flashes up and is gone again; one hears oneself sing a tone that has something utterly new in it. When this single tone has died away, one feels with certainty: this was a message from 'above', the way leads there, and the inner constellation has become a different one from this moment on.

At first, however, one is altogether unable to repeat this new tone; it is, and for the time being remains a *unique* experience. So it remains until, carried by the remembrance of the event, one has striven long and hard to recreate the conditions of its birth, in order henceforth to retain it consciously and voluntarily. And then one day, after a day's work which can only be compared to that of a day-labourer, one is permitted to feel the last resistance yielding, and the 'goal' is reached. Then, however, one also realises that this goal immediately becomes the basis for new work.

Patience, lots and lots of patience is needed! It is the earnest work itself that gives the greatest satisfaction; for one feels oneself deep within an organic process of becoming, in a real condition of maturation. Permeated with this consciousness, one steps happily from stage to stage, while struggle, attainment, and renewed efforts continually succeed one another. In the bottom of the wrestler's soul they create a fundamental atmosphere which alone bears the burdens: a fundamental atmosphere *that relates to the origin and essence of the task* which the artist receives through higher reality.

* * * * *

In the art of singing, the starting point for all teaching can only be the teacher's own ability; for right learning in singing is based essentially on the capacity of imitation. Important though correct doctrines are, theoretical didactics can only be of secondary importance.

As was mentioned in the beginning, the first task, and at the same time the task of most all-encompassing importance for the developing singer, is to master the art of true *listening*, the development of the inner ear. This is to be acquired in learning to listen to one's own tones as if another person were singing. In other words, one must make the tone-experience *objective in a double sense*.

This may be easy to say, but it is not so simple to do. For, by 'objective tone-experience' we do not mean the mere ability to listen to oneself (which is sometimes not so difficult), but rather that one must reach what is objective in the tone.

When one listens deeply and selflessly to the tone, it reveals a substantial property which before escaped the hearing. As the organ of perception, the ear, takes in this quality again and again, the quality will begin — and this is of extremely great significance — to undergo a process of intensification. And one learns in this way to see that the tone can manifest itself in two ways, subjectively and objectively.

If the 'objective experience of the tone' is still unknown, one will scarcely grasp what is really meant here. However, once perception of the objective tone (or more exactly, of the objective in the tone) begins to set in, one experiences how the slightest subjective influence colours the tone. When this happens, it is as if the tone were covered in a veil — it is a 'captive'. And in this sense all tones are captive that are produced by people who sing out of their organism. These singers identify themselves with the tone; for them, the tone is something human.

45

Whoever penetrates to the objective tone, however, gets rid of the coverings, the hindrances that surround it. He frees it from its prison; he can follow the striving of the freed tone and let himself be borne by it.

If we look for a suitable definition for this new, ideal tone, saturated with sound-substance, we must call it the *'dematerialised* tone'.

To master the art of objective listening is in actuality not so easy, for the listener must be willing to give up a certain subtle form of egoism: he may no longer wish to 'enjoy' his tones, no matter how beautiful they are.

Once, however, one has attained the objective tone and can bring it forth at will, then it begins to come alive and reveal itself in its true nature more and more. It becomes 'essential'.

Here, we speak of the living essence which has its *outward* expression in the sense-perceptible tone. *This* living essence refers back to the supersensible tone-being itself, which lives and creates in the spiritual background.

Now if it must be said that this tone-being — creatively at work in the spiritual background — does not live *in* the tone, but as it were all around it, *between the tones,* then it is not remarkable that present-day singing pedagogy must find this incomprehensible. But it is so!

This knowledge provides the basis on which a very definite law can be established, having a great significance for our school of 'uncovering the voice': that 'improvement' or progress will not come about through a long holding of the tones, but rather through beginning and ending the tone again and again. For the actual contact with the essential aspect of the tones occurs in the toneless silence between cessation and renewed attack in singing.

To be sure, with the currently accepted notions one will not find easy access to a fact such as this. Through spiritual investigation, however, it can be explained. Spiritual research shows us that the tone-being, which we came to know earlier as the archetypal voice, can be understood through supersensible research and perception as an essential active principle. The tone-being is like Goethe's 'Urpflanze', which can be grasped and perceived through intuition in its archetypal form, and yet through supersensible perception can be found again in a higher sphere as a being, active in reality. Thus this tone-being, like Goethe's 'Urpflanze', is an entity which exists always. The 'voice', after all, is not a material thing that functions only in the moment of tone-manifestation and evaporates into nothingness between the individual tones; the voice has an eternal existence, and therefore one can make contact with it even when it is not manifesting itself.

This 'general' or archetypal voice, which gives rise to the different kinds of voices through its encounter with human bodies — like the 'Urpflanze', which brings into existence the different species of plants through its encounter with the earth — represents a capacity in permanence. This is a fact, although admittedly it is as easy to see theoretically as it is hard to employ practically.

But it can be felt from this that one must conduct one's study with two views, as it were. Certainly one must practise — in fact, one must work almost like a lumberjack; but one must also develop a spiritual instinct to leave time for the creative, to provide the conditions for the work which goes on *unconsciously* for the human being. That is, one must be able to sing when necessary and keep silence when necessary; for the actual processes of transformation — as everyone will confirm from his own experience — take place in the *night*.

It is not uncommon that *before* this kind of schooling, the singer experiences definite difficulties of a completely

47

personal nature – depending on his particular organisation – while working on the tones. In the course of this schooling, however, these difficulties slowly take on a different, ore *general* character, so that in the end they show themselves to be of the same kind for all singers, at least to a great extent. And when the tones begin to free themselves from the organic constitution, one experiences more and more how all tones assume and retain a quite individual character.

The fact that 'individuality' can be attributed to every tone in the scale is known to every musician of fine sensibility. Absolute pitch, for example, the ability to determine key and tone, rests solely on the gift of sensing the unique quality, the 'individuality' of the keys and tones. However, the individual character of each tone cannot unmask itself to the singer until he has overcome his subjective relation to the tones. On the other hand, once he meets the tones in their own life, he experiences their inner quality; then it is natural that his experience and the experience of other singers are alike.

So, to a certain extent the difficulties assume a more general character when they are in the objective realm. For example, it would be natural to assume that a high C being worked on in the school of uncovering the voice would be easier for a soprano to 'realise' than for an alto. But it is not so. The difficulties in releasing the individual tones – which represent at the same time the difficulties in objectifying them – are to a high degree alike for all human beings, provided no particular organic impediments are present. In fact, it is found that these difficulties repeat themselves on the octaves. For instance, when the tone C' has changed through practice, a change has also come about with C'', only not so fully. Thus the octave-tones influence one another. This as it were uniform transformation of the tones simply points to the unity-principle of the tone-being, to the archetypal voice. This sounding entity, which manifests itself in all tones as sound-essence, as a characteristic-general quality, is in fact that mysterious creative 'something' that gives the tones their likeness; it brings the tones, which before 'uncovering' appeared as single manifestations of the human organism, into an ideal system which the artist can then use for his true purposes.

A perfected human voice is a living organism (a 'voice-organ') which can simply only be grasped in inner perception. The members of its being ('Wesensglieder') are the mysteriously interconnected tones, which are endowed with the ability to lend one another their powers. Thus it becomes understandable that when the higher tones are worked on, the lower ones 'disappear', that they temporarily weaken, and vice versa.

All of this indicates strongly that there must be an essential common element, an active 'stream' which carries all tones, can contact all tones, and has the desire to manifest itself in all tone-forms. *This 'stream', the sensibly audible image of the tone-being, this living, essential quality in all tones is the Sound, to be clearly distinguished from the tone.* On the current of the sound we can reach each single tone, hold it, transform it, and finally bring it to fit in perfectly with its brothers and sisters like beads in a necklace.

It is our hearing-organism* as a whole which forms the tones by means of the sound; and the throat — along with its associated organs — is the instrument of the tone-forming organ. Similarly, it is not the fingers that play the violin; rather, the inner listener in us plays the violin by means of the fingers. Perhaps still more correctly: the soul, through the hearing-organism, plays the instrument.

*See Afterword.

49

The basic experience of what is new in the school of uncovering the voice is just this experience of the sound, which discloses itself to the human being in its *true* nature only on the basis of a new direction of research and a new explorer's sensibility. The sound, like a living being, takes over the direction and begins to form and trans-form its instrument (the throat, ears, respiratory organs, and in addition the speech organism, which will be discussed later). In this way, in the course of the schooling it can pour itself more and more into the individual tone-vessels as a precious essence, as a sound-substance which finally fills them to the brim.

Now one almost tangibly grasps the creative power of the tone-being. Out of these experiences, a feeling of reverence grows towards that which is removed from human volition, towards that which lives and weaves beyond the personal will of the artist, always ready to communicate itself to the singer when he creates the conditions — both organic-physical and moral — for it.

To be sure, this first great success in the school of uncovering the voice is hindered by mis-formed and diseased organs. The organisation as a whole, and thus into the laryngeal organisation (not to mention yet the speech organisation) is, after all, generally quite hardened. The ear, especially the inner ear, almost always hears badly in our times. And the consequence of this is that it can no longer give the right 'command' to the larynx — command it to dispose itself in such a way that the sound can engage creatively from 'above'. Our whole hearing-organism is dull, the larynx inelastic, and the whole process is clouded and blurred by an irregular, unwholesome respiration. And yet the creative power of the sound prevails over all these imposing hindrances! It is not only an artist; it is also a healer!

50

Thus, at this stage we have a threefold distinction to make; we are dealing with three elementary factors: First there is the being of tone, the archetypal sound, which contains in itself the possibility of manifesting all sensible tones (it would naturally be a terrible mistake to picture this *one sound* singularly, after naive analogy to that which issues from its being: a single, sense-perceptible tone). This *one sound* is the unity, the choir of all that makes tones, in a creative-essential, supersensible, archetypal form.

Second, there is the sound element connected with all human vocal manifestations, the essential element which is more or less clearly perceptible as the characteristic-general quality in all human tones. This second factor, which can be felt as the earthly representative of the divine tone-being, is the chief factor in the practical study and in the art of singing. The correct understanding and use of it is the critical condition in all true striving. However, it will be significant whether one stays with this primary element (which Bruns also clearly perceived), or if one moves beyond it to the tone-being — that is, not the sensible tone-essence, but the spiritual archetypal sound which exists *behind* this tone-essence. It is this which determines whether one has a sensory or a spiritual relation to singing, and all the consequences which flow from this.

Third, there are the notes and their coloration — the aspect of singing that bears the most obvious stamp of the natural.

However, in singing we are not dealing just with the pure sound element; the element of the sounds of speech (see Translator's Note) also comes into play in very close connection to it. The latter, however, is most dependent on the individual, natural aspect of the singer's speech-organs. This applies of course to the speech sounds insofar as they are connected with singing, and not to speech itself. After all, tone-colour or timbre, in contrast to the sound element and the tone-being, is not a general aspect, but a personal element in singing. These tones and their beautiful coloration are in fact what one accepts as 'voice' or 'singing'. (See following chapter.)

As the creative force of the sound engages into the organs (these two represent polar opposites), the organs and their functioning become easier for the singer to sense and observe. And through such a power of observation refined by the sound-experience, certain physiological facts are discovered. These facts are extremely significant for a *comprehension* of the processes within the schooling (but not for the practising itself); and once they have been spoken of, they simply cannot be left unconsidered. The following explains what is meant.

Natural science really knows relatively little about the physiology of singing. Of course, it seeks with the outward means at its command to clarify both the functional aspect of singing as well as the mystery of the human voice in general; but it will never fathom these secrets on the path it has taken. Only if it could raise itself to a science of the living, only if it could 'slip under the skin' of life, in order to conduct its observations *from the inside* — only then could it hope to get close to the mysteries it seeks. However, the representatives of such a future science would have to be artists, too — and not just singers in the usual sense of the word, but singers who can feel their way into the web of the living. Then — only then — very much about the physiology of singing, especially in relation to the larynx, would be unveiled to it.

We know of two vocal cords of the larynx, but we know very little about how singing makes use of those two vocal cords. The following discovery is made in the school of uncovering the voice.

We speak and sing mainly with the right vocal cord, while

the left, in our time, is condemned to be a more or less dumb 'spectator' (or listener) of the right one.

The right vocal cord is somewhat thicker than the left. It is possible not only to sense and observe the activity of the two vocal cords, but also to gain control over them, so that the left cord can be voluntarily included or excluded from participation. When the left vocal cord is included in singing, the pitch rises somewhat, because this cord is more delicate, 'thinner'. It acts like a thinner string on a stringed instrument: raising the tone.

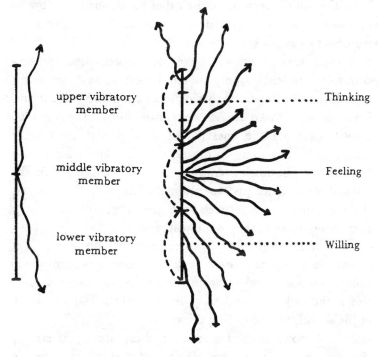

Now, with concentrated practice, the following peculiar fact is found: one has the sensation as though the vocal cords lay vertically, and not horizontally as anatomy reveals.

(It must be pointed out that the school of uncovering the voice has no intention to evoke this typical experience. Such a fact will merely be mentioned for the student's orientation.)

, Furthermore, it is learned that the right vocal cord is divided into three separate vibrating regions, while the left is divided into only two. Thus, the two vocal cords stand in a vibratory relation of 3:2 to one another.

Close observation of the right vocal cord shows that its upper region sends all vibrations in an upwards direction.

In the middle region, on the other hand, one half vibrates upwards, the other half downwards; and from the third region all vibrations flow down.

These three 'regions' have developed their .present vibratory tendencies only in our times; in past times this was different. Hence, a sort of separation and 'transitions' have arisen. What singer does not know the dreaded transitions from the chest tones to those of the middle range, and from these to the head tones! The basic reason for these embarrassing transitions must be sought in the physiological facts just mentioned. The vibrations of the three regions no longer pass so organically, so fluidly from one to the other as they did in earlier times.

To repair this damage (we need not explain here how it arose), to bring the three separated vibratory centres to flow into one another again — this is no easy task; yet this is the task that makes up one side of the essential work in the school of uncovering the voice.

In addition, it is found that these three differently vibrating parts of the right vocal cord stand in a certain inner relation to the whole human being, insofar as he is a being of thinking, feeling, and willing. One could also say, insofar as he is a being of head, chest, and limbs, since the upper vibratory region of the right vocal cord relates to

54

man as a thinking being, the middle region to man as a feeling being, and the lower to man as a being of will.* (This will be discussed later in greater detail.) In view of this inner dependence between the physiology of the right vocal cord with the physical, soul, and spiritual nature of the whole human being, this school naturally must deal with this fundamental relation in a threefold way. First, through thinking, i.e. with thinking as a basis and working factor; next through the feeling; and thirdly through the willing.

In this way, three different phases develop in the schooling, each different from the others as thinking, feeling, and willing actually differ from one another as activities of the soul.

These three different phases in the school of uncovering the voice can best be designated according to the chief task which they set us:

Phase I: 'Direction of the Sound': Finding the direction for the sound stream. Here we deal chiefly with the conceptual element as a helping factor.

Phase II: 'Expansion': (the meaning of this will be discussed later). Here the element of feeling is the essential aid.

Phase III: 'Reflection': (also to be discussed later). Here it is necessary to call up an activity of the will element.

*In this naive-empirical way, we arrived independently at the three-fold physiological division of the human being.

Chapter Two

MUSICAL SOUND AND THE SOUNDS OF SPEECH: TWO ESSENTIALLY DISTINCT WORLDS

In the first chapter of this book on the uncovering of the voice, we have presented mainly general considerations and guidelines; and now we would like to try and describe the essential substance which confronts one as a practical task on beginning the schooling.

Before going into the primary element in singing, the sound world, it would be useful to speak of something which is the most important point of departure for the practical work: the *difference between the world of sound and that of the speech sounds*, as well as the fundamental attitude that the singer must take towards these two factors of his art. We shall also speak of the difference between sound and the musical tones, which is of eminent importance for a knowledge of the singing functions.

To many people of the present, the concepts of *musical sound* and a *speech sound** have become so undifferentiated and indistinct, that in common usage they are hardly distinguished any more. Hence it is not surprising that nothing is properly known any more about the exceedingly important fact that (musical) sound and the speech sounds are in reality *representatives of two different worlds*.

Moreover, when one hears how the concepts of tone and sound* are used, one gets the impression that there is

*German: *Klang* and *Laut*, *Ton* and *Klang*. See Translator's Note.

56

scarcely any essential difference between them for most singers and singing teachers. To them, tone and sound appear to be the same; and yet it is of such importance whether or not one comes to a clarity about these concepts — and it is no accident that they are individual concepts.

For the art of singing, in any case, it is simply catastrophic that consciousness for these things has been lost! Then the singer no longer has the possibility of orientating himself rightly in applying the elements of his art.

In the first chapter we spoke again of sound and tone, but without differentiating exactly between the two concepts. For a real understanding of this school of uncovering the voice, however, it is absolutely necessary to see the completely distinct nature of tone and sound manifestations, without this insight as a basis, much of what is to be said would simply remain floating in the air.

A tone can be spoken of as having little or much sound, as 'soundless' or 'sound-full'. The same tone, sung by different singers — or by the same singer but in different dispositions — can 'sound' more or less.

Figuratively, one could most accurately picture each tone as a form, a vessel, having a relatively independent existence. This form or vessel has of itself no actual content, but gives to the sound poured into it the characteristic colouration or timbre determined by the singer's organism. It is like a vessel into which water is poured: it will form and colour the liquid according to its own form and colour. So the tone, or figuratively speaking the tone form, offers itself to be taken and filled by the sound stream.

In truth, the singer wrestles each moment for this very aim; to fill out his tones with sound, i.e. to fill up his tone forms with substantial content. And that which the layman calls 'voice' is in reality nothing other than this characteristic personal colouration of the tone. It is this personal, natural aspect of the voice which to him sounds beautiful or not, and by which he judges the 'value' of the 'voice'.

In actuality, however, to the degree that a tone manages to appear in sound, to be saturated with sound, to that degree it objectifies itself, freeing itself more and more from this personal organic colouration. It is quite right to state: if a tone is poor in sound, this is due to its material bondage; the materially released tone, on the other hand, is sound-fulfilled. Thus the sound-fulfilled, materially unbound tone and the 'objective' tone are one and the same concept.

From what was said about this in the first chapter, it is found that an 'objective' kind of singing signifies a constant touching with a super-personal reality; that is, the stream of power from the supersensibly sounding world flows continually into the tone forms in this kind of singing.

However, the singer who lacks the experience described by these words, whose singing has never been saturated with sound, will be able to have only a very imperfect conception of the true sounding of the tone. And when such a kind of singing first meets his ear, it will be a great surprise, and may even put him off.

At the beginning of his schooling, the student can only grope towards this experience of sound; yet his ear will slowly awaken to the novelty of it, when his own tones begin to be filled with the objective sound stream. In practice, all those who succeed in saturating their tones with this sound substance show a certain likeness in the sounding of their tones. It was this fact that first enabled us to recognise the inner lawfulness of the sound principle, since sound can manifest itself through the most various human organisations existing.

The objective tone *always* makes its presence known through its silvery sound, a sound which is not really related to the human organism. It has something 'spherical' about it; it is as though the sound came not from the singing organism, a single point in space, but from the whole *space* surrounding the body.

Now let us proceed to the distinction between the concepts of (musical) sound and speech sounds. From what was presented in the first chapter, we have been able to recognise (musical) sound as the unconstrained flowing principle. The speech sounds, on the other hand, we must describe in terms of the *plastic* principle, the principle of conscious moulding and forming.

Here it should not be hard to see that a sort of polarity is revealed on the functional level itself.

As one searches and researches in the way described at the beginning of the book, letting oneself be carried and led farther by the phenomena themselves, the experience of this functional polarity will practically force one to realise that the singer's orientation towards these two factors must also be a polar, a dual one.

Once the singer has opened the right paths to the sound stream (see following chapter), he must assume a rather passive posture towards its will to flow; he must retreat with his own will and feeling, simply in order to give the sound stream free rein. On the other hand, the nature of the word, the plastic-creative principle, calls forth the *active formative forces* — and to the utmost degree. This, however, means that one must begin to work with the greatest energy on the imperfections of one's own physical speech organisation, in order somehow to reach the musculature of the tongue and lips, the jaws and palate, etc. One must send formative will into those provinces of the speech organisation that are hardened, deformed, and therefore partly removed from the formative force, so that perfected plastic forms are achieved (see chapters 6 and 7). For, only through forms that are plastically

59

perfect can the speech sounds manifest their essence in its purity and truth.

Thus, for example, an I, Ü or U sung on high C and sounding more like a formless A; a lisped S, a velar R or L — these are no pure, true sounds! They come from distorted, unmastered forms. The formative force cannot reach to the particular muscle group which should produce the correct form; in other words, because of the organic make-up of the tip of the tongue, it cannot accept the formative will, so to speak — it does not react. Then, to make up for this, other muscle groups not originally intended for this step in; for the speech organisation in man is full of wisdom, and can always help itself somehow. In this way an S sound does arise, but a lisped one, and so forth.

To get a practical experience of what is meant here, all one need do is to vividly imagine that one is standing face to face with a completely deaf man, to whom one must communicate some important message. There would be no use in speaking or whispering; one would simply have to try and form the words, syllable by syllable and sound by sound, as slowly and emphatically as possible, in a clearly visible way, solely by *moving the organs of speech*. If (because the deaf person did not understand) one repeats this two times, three times, all the while observing oneself sharply, then one will realise how the active, forming will-force unites with the organs of speech more and more. In the end one can experience the single sound forms as strongly as if the whole human body were the clay of which a creative being moulded the sound configurations. At the same time, one will sense more or less pronounced hindrances everywhere, and parts of organs which refuse to operate.

Such an experience can be of vital importance for a thorough understanding of this forgotten truth: that in singing, once a person has worked his way to the objective sound world, he must adopt a *passive, expectant, observing attitude towards its will to flow; towards the form-world of speech sounds, in contrast, he must bring his active powers to bear in the most intensive manner.* (This will be discussed in greater detail in chapter 6.)

However, we have not only totally lost knowledge of this fundamentally important law of correct singing, but we have actually turned it *into its opposite.* In the kind of singing generally practised today, we strive to approach the sound world actively with our powers of feeling; we press the sound more or less consciously into our physical organs, while withdrawing more and more passively from our speech organisation.

It grows more and more uncommon for singers to make purposeful efforts to reform (or 're-mould') the tongue, lips, etc., to the point where they permit a clear and *unfalsified* rendering of the text. On the other hand, we force our breath violently into the sound stream, 'forming' it and 'damming' it up.

In reality, this fact represents one of the chief causes for the rapid decline of singing ability in our times!

This can be understood as follows: When one works actively on the breath or sound stream, i.e. holding or pushing it (see chapter 9 on the art of breathing), this will always produce an increased supply of blood to the larynx and, especially, to the vocal cords. However, when the latter are over-filled with blood, they become sluggish and inelastic, and no longer react to a 'gentle attack'. This makes one use more force, i.e. heightened pressure, to set them in action again; and so the hyperemia increases and increases until actual organic damage begins, with its sad consequences; a ruined voice, chronic hoarseness, nodules on the vocal cords, etc.

If, on the other hand, one turns the active force towards speech formation, towards the activity that takes place in the tongue, lips, jaws, etc., one becomes more aware of the actual formative agent, as well as of the possibilities of movement of these organs. And thus, formative forces grow in us, along with new capabilities for moulding the speech-sound forms.

Today we are on the way towards forcing the activity of our laryngeal organs into the realm of our volition, when properly their activity should stay completely outside of our consciousness if these organs are to remain sound. In return, we are letting the activity of our speech organisation slip more and more out of consciousness. To a certain extent, we use the function of the sound principle to form the word, and we channel an activity into our laryngeal organisation which should only serve the formation of words.

Through this confusion, our speech — the so-called text — has come into a kind of sharpened opposition to the sound principle.

It was not so in earlier times! If we could look back into very old time periods, we would find that people spoke and sang in quite another way than we do today. Then, in fact, there was hardly any distinction between the two arts — singing and speaking. Speech was in a way a kind of singing, singing was at the same time speaking. (See Rudolf Steiner's writings on speech formation.)

When, for example, one looks at the last spare remains of the ancient secco recitatives that have been handed down, it can still be faintly sensed how the speech-sound element, the word, stands in a different, more inward relationship to the sound element than in our present-day singing compositions. The syllables, the text, seem to be lifted out of their gravity; they seem brighter and clearer, as though they were gently breathed or 'sucked' in together with the tone. One feels that the words are brought to meet the sound; and one feels both of them, word and tone, to be *revealed synthetically on the same level.*

To be sure, one experiences the text as though syllable were merely placed after syllable, while the sense of the word is pushed into the background and only comes through weakly.

Compare this with the *Sprechgesang* ('speech-song') as it has developed today in Wagner's or Strauss's works, and one can sense the reverse: such a distance between word and sound or musical tone, that one is to an extent forced to *choose one or the other factor*, since it is hardly possible to unite them any longer.

Thus one is forced into a one-sided approach: to cultivate the sound element at the expense of a true and clear rendering of the text, or to fall into so-called *Sprechgesang*, in which case one must almost completely give up the fluidity of the sound element.

The fact of the matter is that the *word has changed in its essential nature.* It has turned more earthly, more individual. It has become 'sense-asserting', but at the same time earth-bound, so that in relation to the sound element, one feels it as *lying much lower*, as fallen. It is actually as though the word, through a certain excessive strength, wished to overpower the sound element and *pull it down* to its own level.

This split between word and tone, which has slowly grown to the point where today the two factors confront one another as wholly different principles, can never be bridged — theoretically or practically — by today's materialistic approach to singing, which is ignorant of these evolutionary facts.

Quite the contrary! Practically speaking, in the kind of

singing general today, we descend directly to the word! That is, we direct the sound stream out of its original upward path into the oral cavity, in order to fill out the sound forms directly; and then we simply let it slip out of the mouth.

The consequence of this is the desperate struggle with the text, which is too familiar to us all: *we are no longer capable of producing truly closed vowels* — e.g. I, E, U, Ü, and Y* clearly without falsification in the upper vocal range.

Now, as a matter of principle it is not hard to see that when sound and word must operate in the same 'space' — i.e. in the oral and pharyngeal cavities — a sort of battle must arise. By its nature, the sound stream must wish to throw the mouth wide open, so that it can flow; the speech sound, on the other hand — especially a closed one such as a proper U and I — must wish to narrow and *contract* the oral cavity.

In this way a battle necessarily arises, which we seek to avoid by continually making compromises at the expense of one or the other rival. In the end, however, we can only overcome it if we guide the sound stream back *into its own*, original paths. (See the following section.) This will at the same time free and release the speech organisation.

For, when the sound stream is separated from the speech element and guided back *on its own proper paths*, the speech organisation can assert itself without disturbance, and can set about moulding its speech-sound forms. Then proper articulation of the text will no longer pose problems in singing.

This makes it understandable that, in the school of uncovering the voice, it is taken for granted that an I sung

*See Translator's Note.

on high C must be just as perfect and concentrated as on notes of the middle range.

How devastating it has been for our aesthetic sense to hear completely falsified vowels in artistic singing over a period of decades! Our ears have become so used to this nonsense that we actually find it strange to hear a U or an I sung properly on one of the higher tones. It cannot even be said that this unaccustomed sound is beautiful: at first it is just unaccustomed, and we must try to get used to it. In fact, one gets a feeling relatively quickly for the true forms of the speech sounds, and thus also for their beauty. Then, falsified vowels become absolutely repellent! They are experienced as distortions and caricatures of the genuine sounds — as untrue forms which do not let the essential aspect come through except in a halting way.

However, once we have come through the initial awesome efforts, we will gain such control over the whole range of muscular activities in our tongue, lips, jaws, etc., needed for the moulding of all speech sounds that it becomes a *matter of course*. Then we will have the real experience that *the whole of language — all speech sounds — has been won back on a higher level.*

And now one will be able to understand a very particular demand which is central to development according to our school: *the requirement that one must first transform the elements of speech before one seeks to join them with the sound principle to create artistic singing.*

It is possible to accomplish this thus: one must strive to practise singing the syllables and sounds, vowels as well as consonants, singly as well as in all possible combinations, in such a way that they are liberated from confinement in the physical organs. Thus we release them from their sluggishness and heaviness, and they can reveal their true being.

This 'essence' of the word *appears* when it is able to light up through perfectly moulded forms (which must correspond to the archetypal forms of all speech sounds; see chapter 6); and it will light up in the rightly *sung* word on a higher level than in the *spoken* word.

What this means is that we now can really unite sound and word, so that henceforth they can appear on the same level. Because they have been made akin in essence once again, as in former times, the word — the text — can be raised up and brought together with the element of musical sound.

However, this is not enough in order to reach a real and perfect synthesis, which is actually a prerequisite for effortless and artistically true singing. We must first take account of the altered relation in which the factors of musical sound and the speech sounds stand to one another today; we must work on them in such a way that they *stay in absolute balance* on this higher level.

Thus it is not enough that we make them essentially akin to one another; we must also bring them into *equilibrium*, insofar as they confront one another as *antagonists*.

To put this in practical terms: the richer a voice is in sound, the more intensive the work that must be devoted to forming and mastering the sounds of speech, the more carefully the sound element must be brought in, until equilibrium rules in both cases. In fact this will be impossible if we do not first try to create as wide a separation as possible between the two elements. That is, we must take them apart, separate them to the extent that this is possible (it simply cannot be done very radically); then each can be worked on in the way appropriate to it — transformed, re-routed, and finally balanced with the other element.

Now it should not be difficult to understand why, in the school of uncovering the voice, we begin our practical work in finding ways and means to effect a separation between the sound and the speech-sound elements.

Basically, even if certain auxiliary means are needed in practising, this is more or less a *question of consciousness* — just as it will be purely a question of consciousness when we come to artistic singing at the end of the schooling, and then (in the higher tone-range) will have to deliver the speech element over to the harmonious guidance of the *melos,* the principle of musical sound in singing. However, without a real knowledge of all these things and their deeper background, it is simply not possible to build up a new teaching of singing, a way of teaching which really penetrates to the essentials. We cannot help but experience the new state of affairs, the antagonism between the worlds of word and sound; but we know nothing any more of their original, natural realms, where we will have to work on them and employ them. Because the singer in our epoch knows, properly speaking, nothing whatever of all these forces at work, he has lost himself as an artist. He knows little of his *real tasks;* and he also knows little of the means by which he might fulfil these tasks. Furthermore, because he has become a stranger, an outsider in the province of his own art, singing has fallen into the state of deterioration which marks our times. Because we no longer have a consciousness for the following three important facts:

first: that singing is composed of *two* basic elements: the flow of the objective stream of sound, on the one hand, and the moulding formative principle of the vowel and consonant world on the other hand.

second: that the relation of the word to the sound principle has changed in the course of time, so that it must be transformed back again by the singer, and

third: that these two factors — only after they have been worked on separately — must be brought into a state of equilibrium before they can be united. Because we no longer have any sense of all this, an art of singing has arisen which is no longer a pure art of singing.

The kind of singing which is generally practised nowadays ·can really only be called a sort of *spoken* singing. (What is meant here is not the *Sprechgesang* — or 'speech-song' — found in Wagner and Strauss, but, from a deeper standpoint, singing altogether — both naive, untrained, as well as the artistic, trained singing.)

In fact, the fluctuating, fluid character of the factors at work in singing and speaking has made it possible to fall into a double sort of mistake: spoken singing on the one hand, and sung speech on the other.

Furthermore, this confoundment works on, spreading over and clouding our understanding of the individual property of each of the two arts.

Hence it would be good and fitting at this point for us to touch on the basic difference between the arts of song and speech.

After all, the view exists that song and speech — especially the solemn speech of the actor, which is slightly reminiscent of the church litany — are ultimately one and the same.

This is the most fatal error for our times, and simply goes to show how we have lost any sense for the essential, fundamental, and absolute.

No, our present-day singing and speaking (to be sure, it was different in ancient times) certainly belong to *two different worlds!*

When we sing, we are within the element of *musical sound*, in a region *set above* the speech sounds. In the melody, the world of the Musical reveals itself to us; we are in the realm of feeling. We must live in the melodic sound if we are to perform real singing. And when we add words to the sung note — the melos — we are adding something secondary to the primary element.

The melody, or the sound element that manifests itself in the melody, is the ruling principle; it must take the speech element, which we have worked on and transformed, and *lift it up to its own level*. Therefore we must pause, as it were, before the transition from tonal sound to the word. We must know that a *relative* separation must be preserved here, that the two should be kept in loose connection side by side on the higher level of the sound element, instead of merging word and tone into one another, as is customary today, on the lower level of the sense-asserting word.

Speech, in contrast, is the art of the *word*. In it, the speech-sound element is the ruler; this rightfully pulls the musical sound down towards itself, involving it in its own activity.

Now if there are people who wrongly think that singing and speaking are the same, or at least closely related, there are also people who assert the opposite, saying that singing and speaking have nothing to do with each other. However, the one is as wrong as the other! To divide the two arts in this way and demand: the singer should know nothing of the art of speaking, and the actor nothing of the true experience of musical sound — this is to commit the same mistake into which our present-day science has fallen so deeply, splitting up into specialised departments of knowledge. This establishes specialisation here as well, and causes hostile rifts between these two arts. We know that the doctor, as a scientist, cannot come to terms with a diseased human organism if he stays in the world of specialisation; he can come to a true therapy only if he has the will and ability to regard the organism as a whole. In the same way, it is true that an actor — provided he has no insuperable organic troubles — should meet with proper singing, and the

69

singer with genuine speech formation. Anyway, both should try to penetrate into the idiom of the sister art to the point where they experience what is essentially different in each, and what is akin — the meeting point.

For both arts consist of sound and word! The one has the word as its essential factor, the other has musical sound, the melody!

The following is also of interest: if the speech organisation falls ill, then certain of the singer's exercises can be of *enormous help* to the speaker; for the sound stream of itself has a very strong and intensive action on the organs of speech. This is simply an incontrovertible experience; the exercises have shown their therapeutic effect in very many cases.

Of course, the actor learns the art of correct speaking only through his own exercises, which exist today thanks to Rudolf Steiner. However, when particular healing powers must be brought to the speech organisation, then singing exercises can mean a truly great help.

One stipulation must be made, however: *the exercises for speaking and singing should never be combined!* This applies especially for the singer; he should not do speech and singing exercises on the same day.

* * * * *

If one tries to contemplate all that has been said so far — although nothing has been more than indicated yet — and bring it to an inner experience, one will feel that in singing, one is always moving between two essentially different, though connected, arts. Then one will see why the efforts, the patience and persistence, and also the length of time needed for a real schooling in singing, simply must be *counted double*. For in reality one is learning to develop and master the main factors of *two* different arts at the same time. True, the word element occupies a secondary position in singing; but as for the struggle to make the form of each speech sound true and pure, it is a lawful component of singing just as of speaking. (A lisped S or a velar R is just as useless in singing as in speaking.) Thus the secret of artistic singing is none other than the ability to combine these two factors harmoniously, while still heeding their essential differences. In fact, when the work on both aspects of singing has finally overcome *all hindrances* put up by our hardened and deformed organisation — i.e. when all the consciously conducted exercises have led to a natural ability on a spiritual level, so that they now function unconsciously — *then only this one permanent task remains for perfected singing!* It can be said that in the artistic act, the singer brings the objective and subjective elements together.

Actually, the artist will always have to renew his struggle to fill the tone with sound substance; and he will continually have to work to join the word and sound elements together rightly. However, if he has the will to fight through to a clear, awake, and comprehensive consciousness of the forgotten mysteries at work behind both of these parts of his art, he will be able to become a true bridge for them.

To the layman, of course, singing received through the outer ear will *appear as a whole indivisible element.* He will not become aware of the fact that he is taking in a *synthesis* of different factors, which was first brought about by the artist's struggle for the ideal form. He will not realise this unless he has retained the capacity for inner, objective listening, by which he can orient himself quite well. This, however, is a very rare occurrence in our times.

As we have said, these factors naturally cannot be considered as radically separate phenomena. They are very

71

much members of the singing organisation; but they *are first joined as art by the artist.* Furthermore, this synthesis bears in itself all that is really true and beautiful in these two worlds. Therefore, this kind of singing has an effect such that one would like to call it 'spherical'. How could one describe it thus if one did not have an intimation in the depths of one's being that it has its home in the spheres? The description of singers as 'gifted' or 'graced by God' points to a truth. We must really learn to sing by the grace of God, and not out of our material organisation or out of subjective floods of feeling.

Truly, the grace of heaven can reveal itself through human singing — a force that can purify, bless, and heal.

* * * * *

From what has just been said, the question rightly arises as to practical ways to bring about a change in consciousness and direction in the sense described. Hence it proves necessary to reformulate this first and basic task in the schooling, and to do it more concisely:

One must learn to separate the worlds of sound and word from one another, so that one can work on each individually in the way described, and then bring them together as two separate principles, each founded in itself, for the artistic presentation.

However, since we are dealing here with a schooling in singing, not with speech formation, our first practical efforts are centered on the primary element in singing, the sound element. We must try to free this as much as possible from its combination with the speech-sound element, in order to prepare the right paths for the sound stream. So now we turn to the description of the directly practical work within this school, the first phase of which is the 'direction of the sound'.

Chapter Three

FIRST PHASE: DIRECTION OF THE SOUND

When one wishes to describe an organic process, in which one thing develops by metamorphosis out of another, certain difficulties arise if one cannot proceed according to the actual process in its immediate sequence. However hard we might try to report all that a pupil experiences during a long period of training, it would not help to give an understanding. On the contrary, to follow how the many factors and processes weave in and through one another would have a tremendously complicating effect.

Hence, in the following three chapters we shall seek to provide an insight into the path of development in this school, first treating the most important factor in singing, the sound element: i.e. essentially how the work on the sound element · must be conducted in the three phases.

* * * * *

The school of uncovering the voice develops organically out of a single exercise, which relates to the sound stream.

This exercise can be looked at as a germinal cell, out of which a whole organic structure slowly grows, step by step according to a lawful pattern. At the beginning of its development, however, one does not notice what rich possibilities lie sleeping in the germ; yet later the most wonderful and complicated forms and structures become manifest through it. And so it is with this apparently primitive beginning exercise.

In the second chapter of this book, we wrote that our practical work in this schooling begins with the most radical separation possible between the worlds of musical sound and the speech sounds. It cannot be hard to recognise this separation as a primary necessity, when one considers that the singer must come to terms with the most original and essential element of his art, the sound stream; and he must meet it in so actual a way that he will be able to really develop it and direct it on its right paths. This is no easy task, as one realises when one makes an effort to steer it away from the customary direction that it is allowed to take in most contemporary methods of singing. As we have shown in the last section, it is particularly characteristic for today's singing pedagogy that the sound stream is allowed to flow out through the mouth. However, this way of singing, which has gradually become accepted over the last three generations of singers and today is a general and unquestioned practice, actually bears a great deal of the blame for the decline of our art of singing today. For just by sending the sound stream directly into the speech-sound forms — i.e. into the organic nature, which alone may serve the forming of speech sounds — one makes it systematically impossible for either the sound or speech organisations to work according to their proper natures. And so it will also be easy to see that we have necessarily lost knowledge of their true natures, and also that we will accomplish nothing substantial without first releasing them from this mixing and overlapping, which destroys their own essential natures — i.e. without separating them one from the other.

However, since it is not possible to separate the sound element from the speech-sound element completely, it is useful for the beginning of the training to pick one speech sound which is so constructed that despite its speech-sound nature, it can serve to help us carry out this separation between the worlds of sound and word.

But this is not enough; it must also be able to help us steer the sound stream properly, once it has been lifted out of the speech-sound element.

It must be a speech sound which by its very essence, by its innate creative activity prevents the sound stream from going in its old wrong direction, and sends it upwards in its proper path.

In other words, we need a speech sound which, *by the way it is formed,* i.e. how it disposes the organs of speech, closes off access to the oral cavity, preventing the sound stream from going this way and forcing it to find a way behind the sealed space of the oral cavity, upwards behind the nose, towards the sphenoid sinus and later the frontal sinus.

Does such a sound exist? Yes, there is a sound — which might also be called a 'super-sound' or maybe an 'inbetween' or 'non-sound' — that arises through the blending of the consonants N and G. When one sings it together as NG (not as a double sound N and G) and observes the tongue position which it brings about, then one can clearly feel that the back part of the tongue in fact closes off access from the throat to the oral cavity, at the same time opening the way upwards to the nose and to the cavities lying behind the nose.

We have called this speech sound NG a 'super-' or 'inbetween-sound' because when it is worked on in the right way, it is capable of shedding its speech-sound nature to a great extent. It stands to a certain degree outside the realm of normal speech sounds. It is neither consonant nor vowel, but could be experienced as a bridge from the consonantal element to the vocalic, or vice versa. It is as though the consonantal and vocalic elements merged together on a higher level when the NG sound is properly sung. It must be noted that to correctly grasp the essential nature of this sound, one will have to practise the appropriate exercises and observation for a rather long time. It is by no means available right at the start of practising; it develops its true nature only through exercise. However, once one is able to form this sound properly, one has a sound of speech that stands above, or *apart from,* all the others. In this combination NG, the formative tendency of speech sounds combats least with the principle of *musical sound,* leaving it relatively free; so that, when the sound stream combines with this 'inbetween-sound', the sound element can come through in the greatest possible isolation and purity from the speech-sound element.

Taking this 'more-than-speech-sound' as the starting point for the practical work, one reaches what we have described as the first task in this method: one gradually learns to separate the word element from the sound element, insofar as this is possible. Experience teaches us that this separation is considerably facilitated if one knows how to shut off or exclude the organs belonging to the speech organism — lips, jaws and teeth, *tip* of the tongue (the back part is already held fast by the NG sound as a sort of 'door-keeper') — and prevent them from any active participation in forming the speech-sound. One way to do this is to clench the molars together and press the tip of the tongue against the gums of the lower front teeth. (Further details of this exercise need not be given here.) Thus one can experience much more vividly the characteristic difference between the worlds of word and sound: between the active formative will, which is allowed to play itself out in the biting of the teeth and pressing of the tongue, and

77

the peaceful sound stream, which flows along by its own power. This is a critical experience for the singing pupil's further orientation, for now he can palpably grasp that there really *is* a sound stream, and that one can 'direct' it!

If one works on tirelessly at this first basic exercise, which always uses NG as the speech sound, and which can be applied again and again in many variations, one will soon become aware that the amount of sound substance originally available — which then could only manifest the voice in an elementary way — *begins to grow!* This can be observed best in voices which have never been trained according to any customary method, and therefore have not been mis-trained or systematically damaged in some way.

The same applies to people who 'have no voice at all' and have never sung, because the sound stream could not come through properly, and lay dormant.

It is a fact — and can be attested simply through the practical experience of this school — that one 'can get a voice' by exercising in this way. This fact is really to be taken quite seriously; for how often one meets people who sadly report that even as a child they 'had no voice' and were excluded from singing with the group because they were a disturbing factor. And yet often they bore an intense love and longing for some involvement with singing — a longing that often stays with a person his whole life, and can lead to depression and feelings of inferiority if it is not fulfilled.

If one could become conscious of the full scope and implications of all we have said and still intend to say, one would know that all such phenomena in children as 'having no voice', being 'unmusical' or uninterested, should never be a reason to separate the child from his mates. On the

78

contrary, if one would first set such children right in the midst of the sound stream, imbed them in the other children's singing, and patiently do many sound exercises with them, then one would surely find that with enough persistence their latent musicality can be awoken in almost all cases. To be sure, this is only possible if one can, oneself, sing in front of them in a truly right way, which will transmit health-giving forces to their singing organs; then they can slowly assimilate this kind of singing through imitation.

As we have said, this is not just a theory, but has been generously confirmed by success.

This is not the only effect one will notice from exercising the sound stream with the speech sound NG. Today, of course, it is considered perfectly natural that everyone endowed with a voice must acknowledge quite definite, sometimes even quite narrow, limits to his vocal range. One seldom still finds voices whose range includes a whole second octave, the higher tones being more and more lost in general. Here it is really interesting to observe how NG-singing affects these limits in the very first practice session; one can now reach the limit tone effortlessly, and usually far beyond it. Almost in the same moment that one switches the voice by means of NG into the sound stream, the latter shows its healing, regenerating power. *Our interest is in consciously gathering this power in order to open certain paths through our own organisation.* Then the flowing principle will take these paths to send its healing, creatively awakening influence to the parts of the human organism which were fashioned as an instrument for the musical arts.

Such is the essential task in this first phase of schooling! We must see clearly that with an imperfect and badly tuned, or even damaged instrument, we will not be capable of any true artistic performance. Hence our first concern must be to bring healing to this instrument, which unfortunately is in fact damaged. And how? Through singing! As we have said, though, this can only be accomplished if we accept help from the objective sound stream. Obviously, we can only begin by consolidating what sound substance is already present in a voice; we bring it together with the help of our NG sound, until a 'little' sound stream forms, so to speak. This we can then guide and join to the 'great' sound stream which flows outside the spatial bounds of the human body.

So, if we begin quite concretely with this seemingly primitive NG-exercise and listen intensively to our own notes as if another person were singing, striving all the while to be very awake and alert, then quite soon we will experience a variety of interesting things. In particular, we will realise why an 'inherent creative action' has been attributed to this double speech sound.

In ordinary everyday work, one really has a very good idea of where and how to proceed; but here one must discover that with the best will one cannot find one's way a single step further without confiding oneself completely to the direction of *this single speech-sound entity*. In other words, this NG-sound is not only a means of helping us discover our starting point; rather, by its own creative activity it leads us from step to step, and allows us to experience the separate stages of our progress *through itself*. In practical terms this means that we need only practise by singing it correctly, always trying honestly to watch attentively *where it leads us* and how it opens and widens the way for us, and then we will also be able to orient ourselves as to the long-term course of development.

In this way, after quite a short period of practice, we will slowly begin to experience a sensation as though a sort of centre point were coming into being behind the nose — a sort of meeting point of all the tones sung in this way. One experiences the individual tones quite well, but they seem to originate from *one point*; and this point, when it consolidates, has its seat behind the corner of the nostril, a little deeper within the head (see drawing, point A).

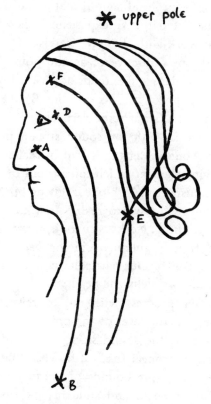

Becoming aware of this point is the first, most primitive experience which this musical speech-sound gives us. As we continue to practise, something peculiar becomes apparent about this point: it has no stability, but remains mobile. What happens is that a certain connection arises between this 'temporary' point and the throat below it; and this connection or 'path of flow' gradually extends down to about the level of the heart and lower still (point B). Along with the downward extension of the path of flow, an upward extension also begins, which makes the point seem . to lie much higher (point D). But this is by no means the end of the gradual process whereby the sound stream takes possession of our head and throat organisation, opening itself a coherent path. We experience this when we simply continue to work with the NG- exercise. Then it leads us to a completely new discovery: as the point moves up, the path of flow widens and extends downwards and backwards towards the nape of the neck (point E). Thus one can no longer speak of a straight or vertical sound path; and the longer one works with the sound stream in this way, the more clearly one understands that in reality one is dealing with a flowing element which spreads out in all directions — a sound organism, to which one is 'giving birth' step by step. However, one will have to realise that this flowing sound entity is *organised chiefly with an upwards orientation*; its activities definitely culminate in the *head*. In any case, at this stage it will be our particular concern to localise it as exclusively as possible in the head.

Now, as we progress with our exercise, we experience another jump in the level of the point (point F). With this ascent, however, the sound stream takes on a completely new and much stronger force of flow, so that now it refuses to be held within the bounds of the physical organisation of the head. or neck, and suddenly begins to flood out through the nape of the neck. Then, in the space beyond it slowly swings out and winds in a sort of spiral as it fades. One can clearly feel this when one has reached the point where the sound stream is pure, and one can properly add the speech-sound element of vowels, and then let the tone appear in the colour of the vowels I and E.

Now, however, the new power of the sound stream takes over the point as well, which then takes on a very different character: henceforth it is no longer experienced as a point. It 'expands' and 'becomes periphery'. Just as the sound-path downwards proves to be a 'path', so what was at first experienced as a point now extends to the surroundings, to the 'walls' which define the 'way'. One gradually begins to sense all the cavities in the head and their walls (nasal, sphenoid, frontal sinuses, etc.) and learns consciously to open access to them more and more.

By now, this originally weak and inconspicuous stream has grown quite considerably in fullness and intensity. It heaves and weaves through all the cavities of the head; and one begins to realise that it could eventually grow to the point where not even the skull could restrain it. So one is not really so surprised to experience one day how the sound stream will no longer be held back by the head, but simply 'breaks through' the skull and spreads out in the space beyond.

Before this great event, one experiences the last stage, in which the vibrations still flow along the surface of the head. It is even possible during this last stage that strange, oppressive headaches set in, but they disappear again immediately when the − now peripheral − point, i.e. the entire sound stream, dissolves its connection with the head.

It is highly interesting that this event can be experienced in two ways: either as if the point were pushing through the limit of the skull, or as if the skull opened and let through the point, the flood of sound.

It is appropriate now to emphasise once again that *all* 'experiences' described here − the capacity to sense such subtle inner moments of metamorphosis at all (for ultimately, these alone concern us) − depend more or less on special, individual gifts, which differ both in degree and kind. It is even possible that the event just described has set in already, though the pupil notices nothing special. But this does not mean that the joy over the event should be the slightest bit less.

So, with the help of this special speech-sound NG, we have achieved the capacity actually to direct the sound stream through our head and beyond it. And now it will hardly seem odd if we report that what we sensed as a 'point' in the different stages of the exercise, now that the head organisation no longer holds it back, swings up to a specific centre-'point' a little above the head. Thus it becomes a centre *outside* the physical space of the body, and accordingly it is not a physical-material point or a point fixed in man's physical organisation, but one present in the *supersensible organisation* of the human being. Thus, this centre is located in that supersensible sound-instrument which causes the material vibrations, and of which we spoke in the first chapter.

To summarise what we have presented so far, we may say: With each note that we sing, with the whole breath-borne sound-stream, in reality we go out of the physical material body and enter into the realm of the etheric world and its forces.

* * * * *

The exercises done in the first phase, which give the sound stream an upward direction and release it from the physical organisation, call chiefly on *one* of the three vibratory centres of the right vocal cord. At the end of the first chapter we spoke of the three vibrating 'areas' as an upper, a middle, and a lower area.

Now in the first phase, one works mainly with those vibrations produced through the use of the uppermost area

84

of the right vocal cord. That is, one uses the upper third of the right vocal cord, and its vibrations, as the organic-physical basis of the work. As the first phase comes towards its end, however, a tendency appears to employ the upper half of the *middle* area as well, whose vibrations (basically speaking) likewise flow upwards, and to mix them in with those of the first region.

However, in most cases, one will scarcely notice that one has reached across the 'boundary' between these two vibratory areas.

* * * * *

Strictly speaking, up till now we have described the tasks and possibilities more or less from the outside of the whole process. To be sure, one will attain real results with this singing exercise through outward efforts, if they are carried through rightly, earnestly and persistently; nonetheless we may not forget the inner relationship of the human being to this work, insofar as he is a thinking, feeling, and willing being. For it is as such a threefold-soul-being that we meet all the experiences in the outer world, as well as all experiences which instigate an inner development in us. And particularly when we devote ourselves to artistic, creative work (whether any kind of art work or, as an *instrument* for real art), we involuntarily strive really to come to terms with our intended creation in our thinking, in our feeling, and in our will — in our whole being. These three powers of the soul become three different aspects by which we orient ourselves on how to proceed in the individual steps of our work.

Similarly, in the course of one's development in this school of singing, one learns that one will need to call on and consciously cultivate these three soul forces if one is to grow into all that this work offers the singer in terms of creativity and self-conquest; for one will need their help to come through the three different stages of the schooling to the desired, distant goal. And this is because of their individual relation, each to one of the three stages.

Here we recognise that thinking and mental representation stand in the most immediate relation to the first stage and its tasks, feeling to the second, and willing to the third.

* * * * *

In the early part of this chapter, we said that we can picture this school as germinating and growing out of one single exercise. Now if we consider this assertion in the light of the unique quality and action of the sound NG, then it becomes much easier to understand. As we have seen, this single speech sound in reality represents the sound stream. It must be regarded both as the 'leader' and the 'way'; and in this light, any approach oriented around composed exercise 'material', as is common today, becomes more or less senseless.

If it is not merely word-play, but an actual reality that the speech sound NG creates and leads the 'way' through its own being — i.e. *if this speech sound, in its activity, comprehends only itself,* then it is clear that essentially *one single exercise must be sufficient*: to let this NG element sound itself, to join it to the individual tones.

This could be done in two different ways: either one composes or takes some sequence of tones — also called a melody — which seems appropriate for the purpose, and uses it as the musical basis for NG-singing; or else one first sets about listening, inwardly attending. If one chooses the latter way and lets oneself be led by the musical sounding of this unique sound NG, one starts to experience the sound stream in such a way that *it forms itself* into a kind of never-ending, ever-rejuvenating melody, spreading out over time and space; and the *separate motifs* of this melody can very well be taken for use in exercises. One could also put it this way: one listens expectantly for the sound stream itself to indicate what melodic aids it requires for one's progress in each stage of the work. In this manner exercises also come into being; but the true nature of such exercises can only be understood by one who regards them as selected 'sections', fragments of motifs of a single, integral, ever-sounding stream of melody. Just as the river, flowing on its way to the ocean, mirrors singly all the changing motifs of its banks, both small and large, so there is an abundance of melodic sections here. Thus it becomes clear to us that while we take one single exercise as our basis, this exercise is itself creative, and gives us many, many melodies.

After some time, we have gradually developed the *essential quality* of NG so strongly in our consciousness that we can carry it over to the other speech sounds, at first the vowels. And once again the sound stream reveals itself, giving us a panoply of new exercises.

Among them are breathing exercises — we should really call them 'exercises for forgetting the breathing' — in which the pure melodic element combines with the element of harmony or rhythm; still, in this phase the *melodic element* always remains the basis on which the entire work rests.

Now, if we consider that in the world of music the element of melody really corresponds to the representational, thinking element in the human being, it becomes clear why we must call chiefly on the power of mental picturing to aid us in this phase. For only essentially related elements can mutually recognise and support one another. The objective, cool current of the melody, removed from the personal world of the human being — which the art of 'coloratura' allows us to experience best — and the cool, sober world of thinking! Who would not sense, even from a purely external point of view, the essential kinship of these two elements?

To accomplish anything at all by concentration, it must be supported by the power of thinking. Thus, if we want to switch the flow of the sound stream from a wrong direction to a right one, we must be able to concentrate on this task, and on the sound stream.

So, if one wants to bring the sound-path higher and higher, to really 'sing out beyond the head', one must invoke the helping power of thinking. In forming the sound organism, the faculty of picturing and observing can help one wonderfully, the moment one concentrates it in that direction.

In fact, there is no doubt that one would not go far if one spared one's energies in picturing and observing, if one were to practise in the ordinary way and wait for things to develop by themselves. Only by really applying one's power of mental representation (See translator's note), so that the *mental pictures* in turn have a strong and lively influence on the organic level and (which is extremely important) can thus continue to work on during the night — only under such conditions does the path upwards open in a healthy way.

To go into this in greater detail would take us too far afield; however, one can find much in physiology and psychology that could serve to explain and confirm this fact.

When one has worked one's way laboriously and patiently through all we have described, and when one has attained the upper free-floating sound centre, then an experience typical in singing sometimes comes about — an experience that could best be characterised with a picture:

The reader may have observed how, when one holds a match above the glass of a petroleum lamp to set it alight, the flame first appears to float freely in the air over it. When one raises it higher above the edge of the glass, the flame unites with it.

As the flame appears floating over the match, so the tone appears above the singer. But just as the flame, though apparently independent of the stick, actually belongs inseparably to the burning wood, so the tone also belongs to the singing human being. And just as one can bring the flame and the stick together and separate them again at will, so one can also separate the tone, which sounds downwards out of the supersensible point, from the human organisation.

However, if at this stage of the schooling one tries to sing songs on the basis of what one has achieved, then the overall impression will not be very favourable; it will still sound very nasal. The nasal character, of course, is present because in the beginning one has to concentrate exclusively on directing the sounds upwards. For, as we have already shown, the first paths that one consciously creates and learns to use pass through the cavities behind the nose.

These cavities are surrounded by bony material and are narrow, so they give the tone a nasal sound. However, these paths extend themselves organically as the work progresses, and gradually the whole head becomes permeable to sound. As this happens, the nasal sound will naturally change. And when the totally different sound substance of the second phase can be joined to that of the first, the nasal sound will be lost more and more, until in the end it disappears.

To be sure, before this point one will have to have mastered the sound substance belonging to the third phase, and besides the entire sound element all the elements of speech as well. For, a beautiful and true tone — a balanced tone — can only arise when the sound principle, uncovered and freely established on itself, is consciously brought into equilibrium with the word principle, mastered in all its forms.

Thus, in a normal course of schooling, one should take up exercises on the speech sounds in addition to the pure sound exercises as early as possible. The difficulties are widely different for different singers, and so the work will bear an individual stamp in each case.

We are well aware that certain questions remain open at this point. However, these questions cannot be properly posed but through the experience of the school itself. To answer them would make it more complicated to present the method itself, and we would like to avoid this complication. Thus, it must suffice here to indicate that we know well the questions that can be asked about what we have presented, and believe that we can answer them.

Chapter Four

SECOND PHASE: EXPANSION

The work of the first phase finds its continuation in our task for the second phase. In a certain sense it is even a direct continuation, although we must realise that we confront a basically different sort of task.

Here again it is a matter of opening a way, a further way for the sound stream. However, in opening this second 'way' certain very definite obstacles make themselves felt: resistance stemming from our organic make-up, in particular from the physiological and functional activity of certain muscles in our body which are primarily connected with singing. These obstacles can only be overcome and eliminated by a tough and canny struggle aimed directly against them. This means that we will have to engage our active powers with the greatest intensity, in order to enliven and re-structure our own organisation. (See also chapter 6.)

This is really a different sort of task than that of the first phase; and yet the essential difference between the two is by no means so great if one looks at the *end result* of the work of both phases, as we shall see:

The 'way' on which we worked to direct the sound in the first phase, lay open and thoroughly accessible to it anatomically and physiologically. We only had to learn to direct the sound stream so that it actually took the direction upwards through the existing cavities of the head and then flowed on out of the head.

However, at the entrance to this second, further 'way'

(which is also very much available), our physical organisation has contracted into a sort of 'door'; and we must now bring this *'door' to open,* so that the sound stream can make use of the second way as well. We will have to apply our active powers to the opening of this 'door'; we will have to 'fight' with our 'contracting' physical organism in order to free the entrance to this second 'way'.

And this second way, where does it go? And where is the door that closes off the way?

Here we will have to say something that will no doubt seem the purest nonsense to a singing teacher sunk in materialistic conceptions. But it *must* be said, because it simply corresponds to a necessity and — a truth:

The second main way for the sound stream leads *from the larynx through the expanded pharynx, through the 'doors' at the mouths of the Eustachian tubes* (which connect the pharynx with the ears), *through these into both ears, through these and out of the organism.*

Just in trying to form a picture of this task, one gets a feeling for the real difficulties to be overcome. Looking at it from a purely physiological standpoint, however, it immediately becomes clear that a certain amount of work must be done simply on the organic level. For without a considerable widening and stretching of the pharyngeal cavity, the sound stream will have no possibility or *reason* to branch off from the larynx into the Eustachian tubes instead of flowing straight up. Hence without such an extension *no solution to this problem is thinkable!*

Perhaps this can best be understood with the help of a drawing. Here we have a symbolic schema of the throat and pharynx; on it we indicate where the entrances — 'doors' — to the Eustachian tubes lie imbedded on the sides of the back of the pharynx.

One must exercise in such a way that the upper part of the throat, or pharynx (point a) is widened and extended, so that this expansion of the pharyngeal walls — which are anatomically directly connected with the apertures of the Eustachian tubes — conveys itself to these apertures. In this way, the entrances to the Eustachian tubes, and to the ears, are in fact opened.

This provides the physical precondition for the sound stream to turn off from its straight course upwards, and branch off sideways into the Eustachian tubes. (Points a and b are then located where a^1 and b^1 are indicated.)

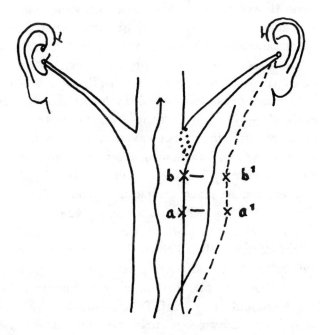

Despite the difficulty of expressing this, it ought to be clear now that one cannot get at these 'doors' directly, but that they are forced open by the general stretching 'expansion' of the pharynx or throat. The point (and once again we are dealing with a 'point') from which one can begin the work of expansion lies somewhat deeper in the throat and more lateral. (We will return to this later.)

It would be natural to wonder if this particular task can really be accomplished. And we must honestly admit that it requires much more patience and also greater dexterity than for the direction of the sound. Very much depends on the capacity one acquires for true listening.

If it were possible directly to reach the place in the throat region that we must take as our starting point, and consciously train it as a sort of gymnastic exercise, then from a purely external point of view our task might not be so hard. However, this whole area, including our target point, is such that (before schooling) it is utterly withdrawn from consciousness. Without doubt, there is hardly any feeling at all for this point, either in laymen or in singers (although singers 'born with a *real trill*', such as Adelina Patti, do in fact know and control this 'point' to an extent).

Nevertheless, everything hangs on the possibility of lifting this point, in the proper way, into our consciousness.

As is known, in the human organism some parts are simply unconscious, immobile, removed from voluntary control, yet can be made conscious and movable through certain exercises: the wings of the nose (which one must learn to extend in the work on directing the sound), the ears, scalp, toes, etc. It is known that with a little practice one can bring these and other parts of our organism into movement. For example, the 'mime' does something of this kind in the practice of his art. To a greater degree than the non-actor, he has gained control over his facial muscles through a feeling-oriented practice; and certain artists (especially athletes) attain such power over certain — sometimes even all — peripheral muscles of the body that they can 'make them dance', so to speak.

Thus, appropriate work will also raise that central target

point into consciousness; and on this basis one can carry out the expansion work described above. This point, as we have said, is 'dead' as far as normal consciousness is concerned. In reality, however, it is not dead, but only unconscious; and, improbable as it may sound, in time one actually attains as natural an ability to move this point as well as the corresponding pharyngeal muscles, as one has for opening and closing the lips or hands.

It would be proper to ask at this point, what speech sound we can use to accomplish this. For this task — like any work on diseases, weaknesses and errors which have penetrated the organic make-up of our singing instrument — is only possible through the power of an appropriate speech sound, whose creative deeds we must follow with our inner ear.

It is the very *same speech sound* — or 'more-than-speech-sound' — *which provided the basis for our work in the first phase: NG*. To be sure, here it sounds very different from the NG we developed in the sound-direction phase. Now, in accordance with its new use, it takes on a completely different sound character: no longer cool, nasal, and soft, but dark and warm, with a silvery ring, swelling by the end of the expansion phase into a mighty, deep fullness of sound.

Despite all the difference between the tasks of the first and second phases of the work (and we shall mention in advance that in the third phase as well, the 'reflection', we use this NG as the basic element), we are able to use this very same speech sound as the basic factor. This shows well that we are not wrong to give it the name of a 'non-speech-sound' or 'super-speech-sound'. It can lose its speech-sound character to the point that neither a consonantal nor a vocalic quality assert themselves in it; but in addition, it also holds back from making any quality of its own felt in the *element of musical sound*. Thus it is suited as no other speech sound to serve the student and guide him in the most universal way.

So, once we have made this new point vividly conscious with the help of our 'new' NG, we immediately cease to feel it as a mere point. (This word can easily evoke the image of something flat and inorganic, which of course is not at all what is intended. In our singing-organism, we are dealing solely with living, mobile muscles; and if we use the word 'point' so often, it is really for lack of a better expression.) Maybe one could put it thus: we begin to sense this point as a sort of 'lever' or 'handle' which we are now able to take hold of and move voluntarily.

The fact that this is possible — that what at first was felt as a point in the organism can change into a 'lever' — is something to which we would like to call special attention. It corresponds to a process to which we must accord a certain *'lawful' significance* in the course of the first two phases of development. With each stage of progress, a certain, slowly repeating 'law' or pattern is at work:

A point develops, *transforms itself, and becomes periphery!*

This fact in reality holds the key to each stage of progress in the singing exercises of the first two phases. Everywhere individual points come into being in our experience, and then grow out, through our work, to the periphery.

Sometimes in practising, two or more circles, belonging to such points that have become peripheral, intersect; then one experiences a sort of break through. That is, one has the feeling that the hindrances against which one is struggling are suddenly broken through, pushed aside, which in our terminology is called a 'breakthrough'.

In relation to the point behind the nose, we said that it becomes peripheral in the course of continued practice.

96

The same may be said of this point in the pharyngeal cavity: it too becomes peripheral; and when this has happened, the first effect will be that we now sense it as a 'lever'. It has radiated such a quantity of enlivening forces outwards around it, that one has achieved a lively feeling for the muscles in its immediate vicinity. And in the further course of this process, the enlivening action will gradually carry over to *all* the muscles involved throughout the pharyngeal area.

As this is achieved, one is also able to accomplish the expansion we have spoken of. The whole throat widens, the Eustachian tubes open — and in that moment the sound stream rushes out through the ear!

This can occur so abruptly (only in special circumstances) that one experiences a sort of shock. For example, this event came about for the very first time as a result of particularly intensive practice, although the exercise was not in the least directed towards this end. For it can easily be appreciated that when one strives to explore in the way we have mentioned many times, one can *never know* in advance *about new things to come.* One only feels one's way, tries to grasp the circumstances with one's inner listening ear; and finally enthusiasm can drive one so far that one actively goes out against 'new hindrances'. And so it happened in this case! Without any intimation of what was to come, but devoting every particle of energy, an attack was quite innocently made on that 'obstacle' which seemed to be asserting itself in the pharynx. Because such a strong pressure was applied, the pharynx suddenly gave way; but because it expanded so suddenly, the apertures of the Eustachian tubes also had to burst open. It was almost like an explosion, and felt a bit like a 'box on the ears' from the inside. The sound waves, running through the Eustachian tubes, struck the eardrum, and one could think it had ruptured! (The experience was actually quite painless.)

When it was shown that this was not the case — on the contrary, nothing in the least unusual was caused by it — it was necessary to try and solve the riddle. After countless repeated attempts, the same event could finally be mastered, and now calmly and voluntarily evoked without pressure; then its significance and 'lawful' character could be discovered and evaluated. The event described — though it occurs differently in each case and also in its separate stages — is one of the most remarkable and convincing in the entire schooling. Moreover such experiences, as strange and grotesque as they may šound, are encouraging and supporting for the student. They mark the stages of progress and maturation; for art, even the most spiritual, always has its technical side, which at its height constitutes real ability.

And now it should be clear why we chose the name 'expansion' for this phase. Just as the first phase was called 'direction of the sound' because in it one learns to direct the sound, so this second phase is called 'expansion' after the chief task with which it confronts the student.

* * * * *

It was mentioned at the end of the last section that the work of this second phase called for the help of *feeling*. Now that we have had a basic overview of what is to be accomplished, it should no longer seem odd that we can accomplish it only with the help of feeling. In our groping and searching for the initial point of attack, we can move towards the place where it lies dormant only through the support of feeling.

To speak about things that can be grasped purely mentally can be relatively easy. However, when one wishes

98

to clothe something in words that take place more or less in the realm of feeling, it becomes difficult to find the right language. Really, one can only describe it in 'feeling one's way'.

Throughout the work on expansion, the power of feeling must be called on in such a way that one gives oneself voluntarily to one *very definite feeling*. One must do this so intensely that it takes place not only within the soul, but condenses into an externally visible gesture or configuration; and this one must *impress even into the facial mask.* Then one will be able to experience *how a kind of interplay is spontaneously established between the particular feeling gesture in the face and the 'focal' point of our expansion work.* Let us try to make clear what is meant by this:

An intense feeling of contempt tends to pull the corners of the mouth down; an intense feeling of amazement pulls the brows up; a humorous feeling draws the mouth wide, etc. Hence, a particular feeling chosen for our work in the second phase brings about a facial gesture which bears the closest psychological-physiological relation to the aforesaid focal point.

Thus the feeling to be evoked for use in the exercise is not chosen voluntarily, but by *necessity*. The student, however, must produce it voluntarily.

This strange process is not at all far-fetched in the artistic calling. The artist, particularly the actor and opera singer, must learn to manipulate the physical organisation objectively, consciously proceeding from definite attitudes of soul.

Once again it is hard to describe what all these words are driving at, given the intimacy of the processes. For this reason, personal experience is an absolute prerequisite for giving instruction. Whoever would venture to give advice solely on the basis of what we present here might commit an offence against the student's development and health. Above all, one must come to a mature judgement as to *how much* of this strenuous work can be expected of the student without causing overexertion and all its consequences. This is why it is so important to train the ear in correct hearing; for the ear is the essential guide.

* * * * *

In the section on directing the sound, we have shown that of the three vibratory centres in the right vocal cord, we use chiefly the vibration of the upper third, the uppermost vibrating member, as the physiological basis of our exercises. (The vocal cord as a whole vibrates in a tripartite way, falling into an upper, a middle, and a lower vibrating member. The further presentation will be simplified if we may use these terms from now on.)

Here in the expansion phase, it is the middle vibrating member that provides the physiological base-element. However, as we master the capacity of expansion, the vibrations of the *middle* member will blend in with those of the *lower* one. They gradually reach over the border into the lowest region, working lower and lower until finally they are produced by the whole vocal cord.

The movement of these vibrations across the border is actually so obvious that it is clearly perceptible even to an untrained ear.

If we now take this task of expansion, in which we send the sound stream out through the ears — i.e. horizontally — and consider it together with what we have just discussed, keeping in mind the *directions* of vibration of the three members, then we can get a fairly distinct feeling for the entire process.

100

We said that the upper vibrating member vibrates wholly upwards, the middle one half upwards and half downwards (taken together, this makes for a basically horizontal direction), and the lower one wholly downwards. Now, inasmuch as the middle member vibrates preponderantly horizontally, it must send the sound stream in a horizontal direction. This is the direction of the ears, while in the sound-direction phase the sound stream is borne up by the vibrations flowing upwards.

From these facts and connections, it seems justifiable to say that the 'lawful' necessity for the two phases we have just treated stems quite simply from the physiology of our larynx and the organs associated with it. At least, one cannot deny that there is an accordance in the most essential points.

And further accordances will appear even more clearly as we apply this approach to various other phenomena in the field of singing, which present-day pedagogical theories cannot help very much in explaining:

Among others, we are thinking of the phenomena of false intonation and what is called falsetto singing.

Singing too high or too low (sharp or flat on a given tone), despite absolutely reliable hearing (i.e. a truly well-functioning ear), is a common problem which can sometimes drive a singer to despair. Despite the uttermost effort, a singer plagued with false intonation is not in a position to avoid singing sharp or flat. If, however, one knows about the different vibrating directions of the three vibrating regions, one will not only gain a thorough understanding for this phenomenon, but will also have the possibility of doing something to help it.

With a singer who involuntarily sings sharp, one will be able to ascertain that he uses *primarily the two upper* vibrating regions, and excludes the lower one almost entirely. This robs him of the vibrations which would balance his tones with their downward flow; his tones rise against his will. In the case of singing flat, chiefly the two *lower* regions are called on; then the top vibrating member is not engaged enough.

It is characteristic of the artist who sings flat that he gradually loses the ability to sing *piano*. He can actually only sing *mezza voce* or the very loud tones. And the latter usually come out flat simply because of the missing equilibrium. The physical instrument does not follow the 'command', the will of the ear; instead, since it is only *partially* activated, it forces the tone down through its preponderant vibratory tendency; the tone sinks.

Here we are not speaking of the kind of false intonation which so often appears at the end of a long career of singing. In this case, the continually repeated wrong way of singing has made the whole vocal cord go lax and hardened the whole larynx.

And the production of falsetto notes? This involves a still further-going exclusion in the upper vibrating region. A kind of division or subdivision arises in this single region — specifically, in its lower half. The falsetto note makes use only of the *very top* of the upper region; and it is actually forced into being only at the moment when the voice has suffered some *organic* damage (slackening, over-tiring, or hardening). Thus the vocal cord must 'resort' to falsetto when it is no longer elastic enough to respond as a whole to the singer's intentions.

Basically, falsetto tones are nothing other than *overtones* brought under a certain degree of control. They arise in a similar manner to 'flageolet tones' on an instrument. It is perhaps not generally known that falsetto singing is quite possible in the female voice as well.

By making a systematic exercise of falsetto singing

in the right way, one can slowly strengthen the upper vibrating member to the point where one day it joins in again as a whole; then falsetto singing is no longer a necessity.

We have mentioned that a false way of singing places the larynx under too much stress; there is too much wear and tear, and the vocal cord begins to lose its elasticity. It is an extremely delicate organ, and is not only intimately connected with man's bodily nature, but also with his soul.

The following few paragraphs may give an indication of this connection of the vocal cords with man's emotional life:

Once the student has acquired the ability, expansion of the throat is experienced very vividly; the feeling even conveys itself to the vocal cord as well. One thinks one feels the vocal cord clearly stretching. But it is not so! In reality something quite different happens to the vocal cords.

It is common knowledge that emotional experiences, especially extreme ones, spontaneously set off processes in the fluid-organisation. Thus, a deep emotional shock produces a fluid secretion of the tear glands. And something *comparable* occurs in the course of the feeling-oriented exercises of the second phase. The material equivalent of what is released by the exercise consists in tiny drops of fluid which are secreted by the vocal cord. And it is this pressing out of minuscule quantities of fluid that gives the singer the feeling as though the vocal cord itself were stretching.

For the singing student it is of great significance to have an insight into these processes. They could be presented in other words, or even from completely different viewpoints. It is, as we have pointed out repeatedly, exceptionally difficult to convey these experiences in words which will describe, both exactly and plastically, the subtle processes set off at the slightest prompting of the feeling or mind.

Flat schemata, sober concepts and dogmatic definitions are basically makeshift aids, and are dangerous! Thus, the schematic tripartition of the fluidly mobile vocal cord is more than primitive in the face of the functional reality observed! Two-dimensional schemata with 'vibratory regions' marked off, their vibratory emanation put in mathematical terms — this gives only an abstract, unreal, distorted picture of the real processes, how they spread outwards *to all directions in space.* Nor is it very different with the terminology used in our school of uncovering the voice! The 'vibratory processes', which one might picture in a simple way on the basis of the diagram, are organically differentiated; and in the course of practice they differentiate more and more. The vibrations do not go like rays out of a point of light, from a material power-source, nor from one little piece of the vocal cord: they naturally *always* come from the entire vocal cord. More precisely, *these vibrations are produced by the singing 'I' or ego on the basis of the vibrating vocal cord.* It happens that only the upper third can be 'switched on' (another *word*), due to the particular make-up of the voluntarily controlled voice-organism. This is why one senses the 'sound-centre' (yet another word), the 'focal point' of the entire complex vibrating process, as being in the upper third of the vocal cord. As we know, the latter lies horizontally but vibrates vertically; and it is able to function only because it represents a sort of mid-point in the whole, complex larynx along with its associated organs. In actuality, the production of the vibrations is a process of the very height of complexity. To facilitate the under-standing, only the essential elements of it can be considered, so that its characteristic functioning in the different stages of schooling can be made comprehensible to some degree.

104

In a school such as this one, words — even the words which compose a science — are nothing more than a means towards developing *dexterities;* they are gestures which try to point to the reality of certain experiences which arise in a 'lawful' way and continually undergo metamorphosis, experiences which one can attain only through *one's own activity.*

* * * * *

So, when one has come to the point where one can 'expand', this means that one not only knows how to direct the sound through the ears at will, but also can control the vibrating regions of the vocal cord freely. That is, now one should be able to move the tone voluntarily from the upper region of the vocal cord down through the second into the third, and then back again from the third, across the second into the first region.

In the process, one will experience something surprising, which manifests itself so perceptibly that even the untrained ear can hear it without trouble. As one goes through the vibration-regions, one experiences the whole sound character of the voice altering and changing colour. Out of the upper region alone, it has a completely other character than when it sounds out of the upper and middle regions together, or out of all three members.

This experience can be the starting point of something important, which should really give us cause for reflection: namely, that it is through this *exercise that one can first understand and acquire true, artistic dynamics in singing.*

It is an actual fact! One experiences, one receives an explanation, how it is that a *piano* can swell up to the mightiest *fortissimo;* and one knows that it is not through the breath, through stronger compression of the air, as current conceptions maintain. They not only explain the arising of *crescendo* and *decrescendo* in such terms, but also teach their formation accordingly.

When one is aware of the true sense of these concepts, one may say with assurance that the *dynamics* in present-day singing have become something utterly *soulless*.

In singing today, the dynamics are produced by damming up, compressing the air — very much like in a *siren*. However, in reality the respiratory process has absolutely nothing to do with true and artistically employed dynamics in singing!

It is even true to say that in a course of genuinely artistic exercise, based on the true developmental tendencies of our physiological nature, materialistic conceptions break down, and mostly express the opposite of what is right.

To fathom the mystery behind a truly artistic dynamics of singing, one must first know the physiology of the right vocal cord properly, and *know how to use it accordingly*. For quite naturally an isolated knowledge of the physiology is of no use. One must first have a sense for didactics and pedagogy, the creative gift for education towards Art; then, on the basis of this physiological knowledge, one must find the right exercises and form them through inspiration, for they cannot be simply constructed.

When a singer brings forth a truly perfect *piano* or *pianissimo*, he is making use of the vibrations produced on the basis of the upper vibratory member. If the tone is to pass into a *mezzoforte*, he must reach down, so that now two members of the vocal cord are in use; and if the singer wishes to move from a *mezzoforte* into a *forte* or *fortissimo*, all three vibratory members must act together as one vibrating centre.

When this *crescendo* all the way to *fortissimo* is conducted in the manner intended here, a tone of unusual strength, intensity, and fullness will be attained. The voice will take on nuances of colouration which in fact can be obtained only when the physiological functions described begin to participate in the 'tone-production' (functions which before schooling were more or less latent, and played little or no part even in artistic performance), and when the opening of the expansion-path permits our ear as well to contribute its creative deeds.

For the human ear — this delicate, complex structure, built with such infinite wisdom, which in reality should not be regarded *only* as a sense organ, but rather as the focal point of a 'hearing-organism' spread over the whole human being — the ear does not just 'hear' like a sort of passive apparatus for registering or monitoring sound (just as the eye does not just 'see'). Rather, like the eye, it should be seen as a *creative* organ. Thus it should be said: As the eye creatively produces colours (cf. Goethe's colour theory and Rudolf Steiner's commentary on it), so the ear also has a sound-producing, sound-colouring action.

And when the sound stream takes its path through the ear, something very special happens to it. Figuratively expressed, it is as though a wise old 'guide' met each and every tone, helping it to a kind of rebirth and giving it a new inner content. For at this moment, inside each tone a radiant nucleus lights up which was not there before.

This shining 'something' in fact represents the first faint reflection of the archetypal sound, which we described at the beginning of the first chapter as follows: When we patiently teach ourselves to attend to the hidden sound, when we make this tone-principle inwardly audible to ourselves — *then the archetypal sound will slowly light up in the outward resonance of our own tones.* And this silvery radiance will grow and grow, developing into a wonderful band uniting all tones; it becomes the 'thread'

107

that goes through the middle of every 'pearl', making them all members of one necklace.

This 'something' also harbours another important secret, of which present-day singing teaching can say very little: *the legato*.

It is this radiant band alone that weaves a *true legato* between our tones, for the simple reason that it bestows *essential likeness* on them. When tones which are essentially alike (in their formation) sound one after the other, the legato comes of itself. Then the singer is not compelled to slur the sound boundaries of one tone over into the next in order to achieve a *legato*, as it is usually done today.

* * * * *

What happens when the tones take leave of this 'wise old guide', endowed with their new nucleus? The question simply must come up: Where do they go, where does the sound stream flow then? Does it dissipate into space, or does it take a path that can still be controlled?

If one would reflect objectively on this question a little more deeply, one would have to realise by oneself that a dispersion of the sound stream into space is unthinkable. For if that were the case, then we would always have two independent streams flowing in different directions. Then the one would continually impede the other, and our consciousness would be 'split' in regard to them. Hence we can only assume that they meet somehow and somewhere.

And so they do! When the 'expansion stream' has left the human organism, it flows up to what we would like to call the 'upper-pole' — the point which we achieved in the sound-direction phase — where it merges together with the 'sound-direction stream'. And at the same time, one begins to experience how, more and more, it is the *whole body*

108

that provides the organic basis for the production of tone-sound.

The reader will remember our statement in the first chapter that the whole human body represents, or could represent, an extended larynx. Of course the larynx (and within this complex organ, the vocal cord) remains the centre for the production of the sensibly manifest tone; but in the end all organs of the human being form one *integral organ*, i.e. the human body as a whole, in which all individual organs merge into one another functionally.

Likewise at the beginning of the first chapter of this book, it was said that the instrument producing the vibrations is not the physical body, but the etheric body of the human being — the first supersensible member of the human being, which brings the physical, spatial body into sympathetic vibration with its inaudible sounding. And one begins to experience this fact more and more in the course of the training; one senses this original source of vibration to be a highly differentiated organism.

Thus, one feels certain vibratory tendencies which push from above down to the diaphragm; in the arms and legs, on the other hand, one experiences the vibrations flowing upwards from below. In short, these vibrations do not simply radiate mechanically out of some kind of central point; rather, one experiences a *vibration organism* in birth, and can determine certain tendencies in its motion — whose limits are not at all defined by the physical body.

Under certain circumstances these vibrations can be experienced very strongly and clearly. After a session of intensive practice, they may occur so strongly in the hands and arms, for example, that they temporarily cause a feeling of cramp. Other, sometimes strange, phenomena can also occur: trembling in the knees, dizziness, etc. But all this happens by necessity, so to speak, and disappears as the organism overcomes the hindrances in itself through the gradual processes of metamorphosis, so that it willingly lets the tones flow through it. For the element of sound, as we said in the first chapter, is a healer — or better yet, ·a *creator!*

As the work in each phase of schooling is coming to a conclusion, this may be heralded by a special experience. Yet it would be hard to give a vivid description of these three peak attainments without resorting to a picture. And so we must use an image here as well for the final attainment of the second phase. It may seem at first unappealing or odd, yet we may say that it expresses the experience *exactly*. For those to whom a statement of the spiritual explorer Rudolf Steiner means something, we do not wish to omit that when he was told this seemingly far-fetched image, he spoke of it as the single possible and fitting one for the experience.

Let us imagine a bat! ... how, as a being of the air, it clings with the claw of its wing to a high-up hanging-hold. Such a sleeping or resting bat is wrapped in its wings as in a coat. It hangs fairly free, completely given over to its element, the air; it does not support itself on the earth, but is released from the earth and its gravity.

When one is given the experience we are speaking of, one feels as though enveloped in a mantle of sound; and this 'sound coat' has a sort of 'finger' or 'claw'. When one sings, it is as though one hangs oneself up on that point over the head, the 'upper pole', while beneath it one feels oneself to be floating free in the air, enclosed in the toning surge of sound.

It should be said, of course, that such an experience, like all experiences within this method, is still only a starting point for further work.

The ideal and aim of perfect singing, which floats before

all important singers no doubt, is that it should proceed completely effortlessly, freed from all physical bondage. And this ideal, even when we have attained what was described, is still far from reached. At the end of this phase as well, if one tries to sing songs, i.e. if one adds on a textual element, it feels as though singing never took so much energy. True, the tones no longer sound nasal; however, while keeping the throat 'expanded', one must devote all of one's powers of concentration to 'holding on' above, in order not to 'fall off' or 'slide down' — as the terminology has developed. And at this stage, it is still quite hard to maintain the expansion of the throat through conscious volition.

* * * * *

Looking back, we can summarise as follows: The results of the first two phases are reached in preparing the 'sounding paths' for the vibrations through the organic structure. One rises vertically to the etheric 'upper pole', the other goes out through the ears and then rises to the same etheric point above the head. We have named these two stages the direction of the sound and the expansion.

Chapter Five

THIRD PHASE: REFLECTION OF THE SOUND

'Reflection!' A concept that will sound at least as strange as expansion. And yet the terminology we use in this school is never meant to be clever or over-sophisticated. The concepts of direction of the sound and expansion (as we have seen) simply indicate and summarise the specific functional tasks which these phases pose. Similarly, the concept of 'reflection' has been chosen with consideration of the most essential content of this third phase.

What does this expression mean in the context of the schooling? To pave the way for an understanding of this, we should like to speak briefly about the process of reflection as it takes place with an ordinary mirror.

When one wishes something to be reflected — e.g., the human figure — two factors must be supplied: first, the human being to be reflected, next the mirroring apparatus. When the person steps before the mirror, his mirror-image appears, thanks to the mirror's inherent power to reflect. Hence, after the mirroring we are confronted with another, third fact: the reflected image. The more perfect the mirror, the more exactly the image will be like the original figure. However, if the mirror is clouded, uneven, or cracked, it will reflect falsely, according to the extent of its imperfection.

Nevertheless, no matter how exactly the image may be like the original, inherently it still can have only an apparent existence. Only the human being is the reality. He is a living entity, and endures; the existence of the mirror-image

112

is short-lived and transient, for it remains only as long as the reflection process lasts.

At the start of chapter one, we spoke of the archetypal sound or 'tone being' as the underlying supersensible entity which manifests its creative activity through the world of sung tones. It was indicated that this entity or 'being' has an enduring character, while the tones are only its fleeting temporal manifestations.

This living process whereby we bring tonal manifestations into the world, can rightly be *compared* with a mirror-image: the creative archetypal sound would be the human being, and the reflected tone would be the human image in the mirror.

Every awareness-process in the human being is based on the nervous system, which functions like a sort of mirror. Which part of the whole nervous system can be involved here? It is the sympathetic nervous system; specifically, that part known as the *solar plexus*, which is embedded in the musculature of the diaphragm and the surrounding region.

In investigating the physiological, organic basis of singing, one thinks first — in fact, almost exclusively — of the laryngeal functions; and this is doubtless all too understandable, for the throat plays the main role in the formation of a tone. It must carry out the 'incarnation' of the supersensible sound element into the element of air, since it produces the vibrations which are the vehicle and mediator of the tonal qualities. Thus it would be foolish to overlook the importance of the laryngeal functions. However, the throat fulfills this task with the help of, and in closest connection with, the reflecting activity of the plexus, the tone-mirroring organ of the sympathetic nervous system.

Although in our presentation of the three phases we must

speak of it *last*, the reflection is actually *primary*, as one finds when one analyses all the processes for their order in time (really an unfeasible task), in order to understand their *functional interplay.*

It ought not to be forgotten that while the development of the sound organism does take place in a certain sequence, on the basis of organic transformations, still the second exercise includes the first, the third embraces the second, etc. Thus it can be said that *in the last exercises all preceding exercises are contained and united in a functional whole.*

This circumstance takes on a special light when we remember that all the great variety of work in the three phases is based on the single phonic element NG.

So we can say now with justification that from the point of view of the *process as a whole, there is only one exercise: that of mirroring! For the totality of all the functional processes as a whole is simply a mirroring process,* which, whether more consciously or less (in fact usually unconsciously), *always takes place!*

It may be the singing of a very small child, it may be 'unmusical' or professional singing – the activity of singing always means a certain degree of reflection. The question as to the degree of perfection in a voice ought really to be put so: *How much 'reflectible' sound does the voice possess, i.e. how much sound which is freed from the physical body, which has been uncovered and released so that it is ready for the process of mirroring?* After all, only something capable of facing the mirror can be reflected. Thus, only what *organ-freed* sound the voice has available is reflected into the audible tones; and according to this amount, one experiences the voice as poor or rich in sound.

This casts light on the organic ordering of the phases of this school; *for in the first two phases we strive to release*

114

*the sound 'organism' from the fetters of the physical
organism, to free it and send it into the space outside the
body, so that it can be reflected from without!*

Some gifted singers — singers with such a wealth of
freshness, elasticity and dexterity that no training could
destroy it — have referred, out of their right feeling, to the
mirror-character of the solar plexus as the essential
component in the complicated process of singing. Caruso,
for example, said that he began his tones from the
abdomen. However, what a gifted singer was able to *sense*,
can only be known in a way appropriate for our times
through a spiritual-scientific approach such as Rudolf
Steiner has given to humanity.

A real *knowledge*, an understanding of reflection will
actually mean far more for the singer than any other fact
in the realm of singing; and it seems to us that its central,
archetypal position in singing asks for a deep contemplation
of it. For this reason we would like to add still another
comparison, one which also deals with an organic process
of reflection.

In accord with the initiates of all times (we refer to
highly developed individuals who experience the supersensible reality), Rudolf Steiner indicates that beneath
all apparent phenomena there lies something essential,
beneath all material existence something of spirit. God as
creator of nature, or 'God in nature', has also been
proclaimed by Goethe and by all initiates as an actuality.

Like the 'outer world' on earth — of which the human
being is a member — so man's inner world also is an
expression of the spirit, and it is so most directly in the
activity of human thinking, which represents a function of
the spirit itself. In man's thinking, a cosmic spiritual entity
reveals itself through the meaningful sound: the *logos* re-
echoes in the human word. Thus in thinking, an objective

115

cosmic being independent of man is manifesting itself. Plato and Goethe experienced this manifestation of the spirit in the form of the *idea as active being*. However, one can go one logical step further and recognise that ideas, which refer through themselves to a being higher than their own, are images of spiritually real archetypes.

Through Rudolf Steiner's philosophical writings one can find Plato's and Goethe's view justified; through his spiritual-scientific writings, however, the step is taken from philosophy to science of the spirit, to a modern knowledge of initiation. Spiritual 'research', as Rudolf Steiner represented it, shows how the 'ideas' of Plato and Goethe can be seen from the standpoint of science: they are earthly mirror-images of the cosmic reality, mediated through thinking.

So, in this case, where we are dealing with the reflection of spiritual reality through thinking in the form of ideas, we also have three elements:

1) The archetype (the essential being),
2) the image (the idea), and
3) the process mediating the image: a reflection process (thinking).

And the organ which performs *this* reflection process is the polar-opposite organ to the solar plexus: the human *brain!*

Word — the manifestation of thinking; tone — manifestation of the ideal tone-world: both are thus reflections of a supersensible reality through a mediating organ.

From what has been described — even if one will only accept it as a hypothesis — one can see that the actual mirroring takes place in a process withdrawn from ordinary consciousness. As little as we can sense or know anything of the primal word, so little do we sense or know anything of the reflection of the archetypal sound. The *actual* mirroring can only be investigated through *supersensible cognition.*

However, this process takes place on the *foundation of organic functioning,* and is connected with processes which project into and also above our consciousness. For this reason it seems justifiable and also possible to use the concept of 'reflection' in a limited, figurative sense, and employ it here practically.

The *outer* processes of this mirroring are accessible to the ordinary consciousness, and it is these which concern us in the schooling.

In fact, the mirroring process is repeated in a certain sense on the *physiological level;* however, this very important process will only be understood when one has assimilated the spiritual-scientific views on the *real* reflection process.

* * * * *

At the end of our discussion on the expansion phase, we showed how the two sound paths flow together at the upper pole, and how through this merging the intensity of the sound increases significantly.

And this is nothing less than a manifestation of the sound entity itself. The tasks of the first and second phases — consolidating the sound, 'peeling' it out of its organic husks — have now been accomplished to the point that the 'unhusked' voice is established in itself and reveals itself as an articulated entity beyond the power of human volition.

For at the moment of this confluence of the paths (and this moment marks the transition from the second to the third phase), the sound entity turns down from its situation above the head towards the reflecting organ, the solar plexus; this it does so decisively that it can be perceived clearly for the first time.

This experience will now give us the further indication we need on how to structure our work within this third phase.

Our task, which we must accomplish through a particular method of repeated exercise, is as follows: We must consciously meet the intentions manifested by the sound entity itself; and we must strengthen them, so that it can reach down from the upper pole and engage fully and easily into the solar plexus (which we will call the lower pole henceforth), in order to be reflected there.

Before going more deeply into this, we would like to refer once again to the relationship of the soul forces to the three phases.

As we have shown already, the reflection phase has its chief physiological base in the vibrations coming from the lowest region of the right vocal cord, which all flow in a downward direction; and this is the phase of schooling which is based particularly on the third, the will-element in the human being's soul life.

In his life of thinking and mental pictures, the human being is fully awake and aware. His feeling-life is conscious to him as in a dream; and his own will-life is actually unconscious for him. It dwells in regions of the soul where man sleeps, which are inaccessible to the ordinary day-consciousness. That is, we are aware of the *effects* of our will-life, but not of the will-life itself.

Of course, the human being cannot voluntarily separate the three soul activities of thinking, feeling, and willing from one another. When we say that the first phase of the schooling is based essentially on the mental life and the second on the feeling, this does not mean that feeling and will elements do not play into the life of mental

118

kind of breathing, one obtains an awareness of the creative, form-giving power of the breath; and in addition, the abdominal and diaphragmatic muscles become stronger, more elastic and mobile. And the elasticity and mobility of these muscles, at the site of the mirror-organ, the plexus, is essential for reflection.

* * * * *

In our work on directing the sound and on expansion, we recognised a sort of fundamental law: that what is at first experienced as a point later grows into periphery. In reflection, we are dealing with a sort of reversal of this principle. Here, the periphery strives towards a mid-point. The work of the third phase consists primarily in an effort to *contract and concentrate so much of this sound — freely moving in the space outside the body — at the upper pole that we create a great excess of sound there.* (We will speak of the conditions which make this possible directly.)

The consequence of this will be that the gathered tone-vibrations will build up a great power of expansion, so that at a certain point they 'burst' out, of their own accord, and throng towards the solar plexus. They will follow the shortest path connecting the upper pole to the larynx. They will rush along the sound-direction path in reverse direction, course through the entire right vocal cord (and one can very clearly hear them passing the two vibratory boundaries), and strike the plexus, which (like an ordinary mirror when held to the sun) radiates them through the physical organism and out into the space beyond.

* * * * *

How can such a thing be done in practice?

Well, supposing we succeeded in producing a sort of vacuum, by means of a completely new kind of exercise: a sort of 'airless' space (not 'airless' in the sense which physics would give this word), a space *so empty* that it contained nothing but a certain 'suction power'. And suppose that by some means we could create this 'void' at the upper pole; then the vacuum would 'suck' in the sound elements vibrating in the space beyond the body more and more, and the 'suction' would hold them there until so much had gathered that the sound entity would *have to* 'break out'.

If this 'vacuum' were then to extend itself over the entire sound-direction pathway, then the sound elements bursting out of this excess would rush down without delay, and — the reflection would be a reality!

The creation of this 'airless' space depends solely on a new kind of *tone-attack,* and on our objective-passive posture towards the formation of the tones.

In the direction of the sound, we hardly paid attention to the attack of the tones in this new sense. We simply went along with the tones, so to speak; we 'directed' them, and won our way upwards and downwards point by point. Now, however, we are no longer allowed to guide them; instead, we must try to remain passive, holding ourselves back to let them arise of their own accord. *The work which we have done in the first two phases is all for the sake of this capacity!* However, for this to become a reality, we must be able to entrust ourselves to the faculty which we have called the one true starting point for true singing: we must entrust ourselves to the attentive *listening of our inner ear;* and *we must give ourselves to it so wholly that we acquire the capacity* (not figuratively here, but in reality) *to 'listen the tones up' to the upper pole!* It is as though we must *intend to receive* them there, to wait listening for them

121

there. This 'listening up' of the tones, or the attack of the tones, is simply a reality; and it is possible only because our expansion work also involves the ear, as we have described, so that we can make use of its now-liberated forces. And to the degree that we can entrust ourselves to the creative power of the ear, we are led *into an ever more objective relationship to our laryngeal functioning. We learn, as it were, to watch over it, at the same time being freed from consciousness of it.*

Here we have the deepest and most important condition for a true and right teaching of singing: we must liberate singing from the physical-organic functioning of our body, so that we only need listen to the power of the creative Logos sounding in us. In reality this must be both the starting point as well as the goal of a school of singing.

And what of the mirroring organ, the plexus itself? Do we have no particular task to transform and 'strengthen' this organ as well, which we have called the lower pole of singing?

No, we have nothing to do to the solar plexus itself. The conscious work of singing practice in general may *never* touch the area of the nervous system. The only thing on which we may and should work (also in our work on the speech sounds; see chapter 6) are the *muscles!* Specifically, only those muscles which belong to our speech organisation. The single exception is the muscles of the diaphragm and abdomen; and even these we cannot work on directly. Our consciousness may never be directed onto the *activity* of any other organ (as is done today even with *internal* organs, e.g. the lungs, kidneys, etc.) We may work consciously only with the muscles of our tongue, lips, jaws, etc. With these, we must strive to develop and strengthen their particular activities; and so we may also work on the muscular coverings of the solar plexus — the diaphragmatic

122

muscles, and in connection with them also the abdominal — to make them strong and elastic. We have already mentioned that this work must take *the form of appropriate breathing exercises* practised from the very beginning of the schooling; for these muscles in fact play a large role in reflection. Through special exercises, one must even bring these muscles to the point where they are strong enough to 'take over the initiative' for the whole process of singing — *insofar as this process extends onto the physiological level.* This means that we will no longer need to attend to it consciously. (We shall not go into details here.)

When one succeeds in this, then, in practising this attack of the tone (at first this is only possible on an extreme *pianissimo*) one will experience how the vacuum comes about. In this way, one has created inside oneself a space where the tone, released from all organic and subjective factors, can appear 'of its own accord'.

Thus the circle of inner, attentive listening is closed, in which we have striven to develop the sound organism.

* * * * *

We are perfectly aware that all we have just said can seem strange; yet though it is not difficult to grasp through direct *experience* or through *imitation,* this is the only way to somehow present it in words. It is simply not possible to show how reflection really takes place. One can only try to describe the essential facts in the most vivid and objective way. In this connection, we would like (although it is more than difficult and could lead to mis-understandings) to report on two strange, seemingly paradoxical experiences or facts which are most intimately connected with this reflection process. They ought not to be withheld, because they can perhaps show the characteristic

123

atmosphere of this third phase in the most immediate way.

To express it radically, one could put it thus: this reflection-path is really not experienced as a 'spatial' path; one has much more the feeling that it is a path 'in time'. It is as though space lost its meaning; for although one is well aware that the upper pole is located above the head, the larynx approximately in the middle, and the lower pole embedded in the diaphragm — i.e. although one experiences all three points as a reality existing very much in space — nevertheless one has the sense as though they moved closer to one another in the process of reflection. The path between them gets 'shorter and shorter'; and finally one experiences the two poles along with the larynx as a single central point. In one's experience, distance, space, is extinguished, and only the *temporal* phenomenon — the reflection of the tones — remains.

Without trying to be abstruse, one could call the experience in reflection a reversal of that in sound-direction. It is not merely wordplay when we say that the results of the phases pass over into one another metamorphically; and this must be reflected more or less plainly in all the particulars. What was experienced as growth from below upwards in the sound-direction, appears in the reflection phase as shortening from above downwards.

Now there is a second remarkable fact to report, which is a sort of reversal of the processes presented as results of the expansion phase. When we continue to observe objectively all that happens in the reflection without our own doing, we can experience the following: what formerly we could only bring about by means of the expansion — namely, an increased extension of the pharynx and throat — now comes about *as if by itself;* and it comes about while the *physical* organ remains in a *state of rest*, i.e. without stretching or tensing. That is, without producing the organic expansion, the *feeling* of expansion arises. However, even more peculiar is that the *effect* of expansion appears in the tone, although *no* organic expansion is performed. The sound-character resulting from expansion is actually present; the sound takes its path through the ears. Thus, while expansion is *not* voluntarily carried out, for one's feeling it is there of its own accord.

Furthermore, as paradoxical as it may sound, this true fact must be said: the throat — now in the transformed state it has come to through the expansion exercises — undergoes a sort of exclusion. One has the *feeling* that the throat becomes transparent, as though one *sang without a throat.*

It is in this manner that the real blessing of the sound-direction and expansion work reveals itself, after all the robust labour it required! For all conscious activities directed at the organic foundation are simply preliminary steps to heal and transform the physiological processes bound up with them.

In truth, the artist is continuing the work of nature when he seeks to perfect his physical instrument through voluntary work. It can well be said that there is scarcely an artistic practice that engages the physical instrument so deeply as that of singing.

To be sure, we are dealing with processes that are inexplicable for the materialistic scientific consciousness, and no doubt must remain so. What can a science based on calculation, weight and measure make of such peculiar concepts as, for example, 'shortening', or 'singing without a throat'?

We also have good grounds for giving no explanation of these phenomena. For the purposes of singing, no doubt, there is hardly need of it. However, like quite a few other matters, these can be satisfactorily explained only out of a spiritual science which measures up to the real needs of the times; and we believe that these pages are sufficient proof that it will be impossible to do without spiritual science in the teaching or the art of singing, now and in all the future. And let these things, though unexplained, be testimony to the disciplined and laborious work, as well as to the unusual kinds of results and 'laws' of which this school must tell. They show how true singing brings the artist into relation, into most intimate contact with the springs of life.

Thus, in the moment when the reflection experiences set in, one experiences the tone as if it were lifted up out of the organic functions, beyond the reach of the subjective will.

At this moment, one experiences a very substantial sound-change for the third time. It is hard to find an appropriate designation for the new character of the sound, other than the word 'spherical'.

One stands captivated before the fact that 'it' is singing in the human being. One steps back inwardly from the sounding of the tones, as from an independent being: from now on one has the tone — comparatively speaking — no longer in oneself, but next to and all around oneself. It is no exaggeration to say: it is as if the human being were no longer singing only out of the point in space determined by the larynx, but as if the space itself — something super-corporeal — brought forth the sound.

Such reflected tones, which move unimpeded through man's physical and superphysical organism, the singer experiences deep inside himself as a 'greeting' from the spiritual worlds. And one has a knowing sensation: such a tone meets the world and cosmos with a totally different effect than the earth-bound tone which is caught in subjectivity. Thus one begins to understand all the weight and dignity of the requirement that we must dematerialise the tone. Here is its fruit!

* * * * *

And now the final experience of this phase: As we have said, an inner necessity demands us to end the presentation of each phase with a picture.

One might have the feeling that the pictures given for the first two phases could be substituted with others, even if one did not know with exactly which others. Here, however, it is *absolutely* certain that this third picture expresses the experience in such a way that no other could replace it.

For this reason it has a deeply shaking character, stirring up the whole human being and striking the soul like mercy and revelation. All that could ever be said of the essence of spiritual schooling (with full awareness we use this name 'spiritual schooling' for the first time) is said by this picture. One can tell *everything* from it.

Our bodily nature is like a dark closet, in which an opening has been left in front, in the form of a living, flowing, gold-radiating cross. One feels clearly: thus the force-streams interweave in the human being when 'it' sings. The 'it' that sings *is the cross!* Standing upright, as if it were supported by or grew out of the solar plexus, it reaches up to the etheric point above the head. In the throat sphere the radiating beams of light intersect, and the whole is like a living organism of sound and light.

It is not a picture to be looked at passively; the singer himself is the picture.

And every human being will be this picture when he closes the circle of development as a singer within himself.

Chapter Six

THE SOUNDS OF SPEECH
OR
THE REFLECTION OF THE WORD

So long as the student dwells exclusively within the element of pure sound, practising tones without any explicit colouration by the sounds of speech (as is of course necessary in the beginning), his real difficulties have not begun at all. This only happens when he moves on to singing speech-sounds, syllables and words.

However, when the time has come to add this speech element to the pure sound experience, he will be forced to become aware that there is a world of difference between musical sound and the speech-sounds. In his attempt to sing music with a text, he will inevitably notice that although he has worked his way to the objective sound world, the speech-sounds will not let themselves be incorporated for a long time. Thus he finds himself confronted with entirely new difficulties, which will call once again on all of his powers before he can overcome them, before he can master and properly incorporate this second essential factor in singing — the world of the sounds of speech.

So now we have to deal with this new, textual element as we have dealt with the elements of the sound world.

There are two basic principles in the world of speech sounds: the vocalic and the consonantal.

As we work our way into them, we will come to recognise that there is not only a world of difference

128

between the worlds of sound and the speech sounds, but that such a great difference also separates the two speech-sound elements from one another; we will become aware that an essential difference lies between the worlds of vowel and consonant as well.

In the second chapter, we spoke of a difference in level which could be recognised in the way the sound and word elements manifest themselves in present-day singing. This discovery is repeated on a smaller scale within the world of the speech-sounds itself: we experience a similar difference of level between the manifestation of a vowel and that of a consonant.

Here, it is the vowel that incarnates on the 'higher' level, while the consonant has more affinity for the earth, more 'gravity' about it. This is why the vowel also stands in a much more immediate relation to the sound principle than does the consonant. Within the world of the word, the vowel is the representative of the musical principle; and as the sound principle is to the word principle, so, on a 'smaller scale', the vowel relates to the consonant. And just as we have to release the whole world of the word out of gravity so that the text can be lifted up to meet the sound principle, so we must work on the consonants until they are essentially akin to the vocalic element and can form a unity together with it.

In order to sing the so-called text properly, we must first learn consciously to place the whole word-realm under the *leadership* of the *vocalic* principle. This, however, means nothing less than that we must *work so intensively on the forms of all the vowels, that out of their own strength they can draw all associated consonants up to themselves.*

Thus we can see how our work on the speech-sound organisation can be divided into two phases: giving form

129

and colour to the *vowels,* which must be brought to such a degree of perfection that they then bring about a corresponding transformation of the *consonants.*

Here one can make the interesting observation that, barring some speech impediment, we generally know better how to proceed in forming consonants than in giving form and colour to the vowels. Thus, there is practically no awareness nowadays for the difference in form and timbre between a dark A and a light O, between a light A and Ä, between a dark O and U, etc. — not to speak of the difficult vowels such as I, Ö, Ü, and Y (See translator's note). In contrast, we usually know quite well how a correct L, M, N, T, or R should sound. Taking this into consideration, it should no longer surprise us that we have lost sight of this fundamental fact: that in reality, *for each vowel there is one inherent configuration which is dictated by iron-clad laws, and which stems from the musculature of our speech-organism.* Our particular task is to seek this configuration and bring it to full consciousness. By their inherent nature, these configurations must be sensed and formed by us with such care and attention that they will call for movement from *all* the muscles we possess, out to the very periphery of our body, including particularly all the muscles of our face and neck. For the *entire* speech-organism — in fact, the entire human being — is intimately involved in the manifestation of each single word and sound of speech. And this means that we ourselves turn into speech forms; we must identify completely with the forming activity.

Naturally, some muscles and muscle groups participate in a primary way and some in a secondary way in the formation of a particular sound. Thus, the *jaw* muscles will be less active in an U-form than in an A-form, the lip muscles more active in the U-form and less in the A-form, etc. But inactivity of any single muscle part will invariably be felt as a hindrance to that being or power at work in the forming and moulding — or at least as a 'beauty defect' in the form.

Thus, our work must consist in the following: *to help all muscles to their appropriate involvement in the formation* — even such muscles as may be incapable of participating (whether because they have not yet been woken up by the consciousness, because they are hardened or maybe sick, or because they are prevented by the rigidity of other muscles).

Described in this way, it may seem relatively easy and self-evident. However, beneath these words lies a far harder task than one might suppose; for firstly, it means that we must considerably strengthen our consciousness before we can 'probe' into the dormant, unreactive regions of our speech organisation, so that we can enliven and awaken them (just how to achieve this will be discussed); and secondly, the capacity to create such new, more perfect forms must become so natural that we no longer need to think about it at all. The forms *as such* must of course be completely released from our consciousness; and this will happen by itself as we come to be able to form them truly. It must simply become a 'natural ability on a higher level'.

When we do reach this point, we will experience a strange and characteristic quality in all vowels sung thus.

And once again we are forced to present something which can only be said in this context, but which must be difficult for a materialistic mind to grasp. Nevertheless, what we have spoken about reflection, taken in connection with what we shall now say about the speech-sound world, should appear well-founded and logical to everyone who honestly will contemplate it as a whole and without pre-judgement.

We get a sensation as though the walls of the vowel-forms were stretching, as though the forms were becoming larger and larger, and at the same time hollower and emptier; and suddenly it enters our consciousness that in reality it is the air, i.e. *the breath which possesses the forming power.* It is as though the breath alone were able to mould the various speech-forms out of the bodily organisation of man. Something of eminent importance has been attained when one begins to perceive this consciously. One then realises that the speech-sound forms somehow and somewhere exist as real live entities, having a 'body' in the breath; and that the breath makes a sort of 'copy' of this 'body'-form within our physical organisation — to the extent that the latter is malleable enough.

However, what we experience as breath — breathed air — at this moment is something other than ordinary air; it is much thinner, much finer and lighter, *as if it were sublimated.* And precisely this makes its creative forming power clearly perceptible to us now.

Compared with our sensation of the vowel-forms *before* this stage, they feel 'void of air'; and this 'vacuum' finally reaches such an intensity that it seems to suck the vowels in from outside the organism. We experience them coming towards us infinitely large, as if from a periphery, out of the great airy world; and it is as if we breathed them in, as if we merged with them into one.

When we learn to understand this clearly in its enormous significance, for the first time we will have grasped one of the most basic principles of a genuinely correct singing teaching. Here, in truth, we have come to the real, deeper meaning of what up to now we have called *'working on the organic nature' of our singing and speech instrument.*

This 'active work' should never be thought to mean that we should concentrate on the movement taking place on the purely anatomical-physical level, or raise it to consciousness. This (obviously) would crassly contradict everything we have tried to present so far. Rather, we must raise to consciousness *this creative formative force and activity* of the sublimated breath within our singing and speech organs — and *not only in relation to the experience of sound* (as we have described in the preceding chapters), but also in the realm of the word.

We realise then that in reality, *listening* plays the crucial role here as well; for only the deepest attention to the creative forming-will of the breath allows it to connect so closely with the physical organs that it can mould ever truer, more perfect speech-forms out of them.

In practical terms, this means that *we must listen to the inner, pure speech-sounds;* we must learn to listen to the elements of the speech-sound world as well as if another person were singing them. And in reality, this means that we listen to how the breath sculpts these speech-forms out of our organisation.

However, this presupposes that we have acquired a truly correct respiration process (see chapter 8), in addition to having accomplished the work on the sound-element described in the preceding three chapters. For, if we are to come on the trail of the true mysteries of singing, we must actually attain the etheric sound level — and this is only possible, as we have shown, through the carrying activity of the breath, the action of the in- and exhaled air. Furthermore, the exercise of our singing and speech organisations must first have introduced its restorative, wholesome forces before we can ever hope to accomplish the formation of the speech sounds in the way we have just indicated.

It is not mere chance that we have been able to draw a parallel between the sound- and word-world on the one hand and the vowel- and consonant-worlds on the other. In

133

fact, this accordance can be found in an even more essential sense: As the reader will remember, we spoke in the reflection phase of how the sound element, the tone, is freed from its organic bondage and weight when we 'listen it up' to that centre which we have described as 'airless'. Now it will be easy to see that we can likewise speak of a sort of reflection of the word — of the vowel — by which it is released from heaviness.

So is there also such a centre for 'listening in' the *word*, the vowel?

Yes there is, in the space outside, a small distance *in front of the mouth!*

From this centre we will experience the 'lighting up' of the reflected vowels, or reflected forms of the vowels!

When we succeed in enlarging the vowel forms sufficiently and bringing them far enough forward *that we can actually include this point in the forms,* then we will experience this second reflection centre. In other words: if we may picture not only the tone-form, but also the form of a vowel as a 'vessel' (the forms of the consonants are quite different) which our breath strives to mould out of the 'material' of our jaw, palate, tongue, larynx, and lips, then it can be said that we must penetrate this activity with our consciousness so intensively that we obtain an *immediate* relation to *all points* composing the vessel-form. Before any form can attain its perfect beauty, without flaws or irregularities, *all* muscles must be mastered to the point that they are capable of *fully* performing their correct movements: movements of lengthening, shortening, widening, deepening, etc. When we have managed to release such moulded vessel-forms, sending them outside of ourselves to the centre in front of the mouth, *then we will experience the reflection of the word, the vowels!*

To be sure, the conditions for the reflection of the word,

and also of the process itself, are different than in the reflection of the sound element: in dealing with the sound, we must hold back all active forces of feeling and will, while the opposite principle must be followed in the reflection of the word. Here there must be a struggle of the breath against the organic obstacles it meets in moulding, here we simply cannot be too active; for it must be evident that we can only attain such a complete mastery over our muscular activity by work actively performed and willed.

However, *the process of reflection in itself* is far more difficult to understand, and also to describe. Perhaps it could be said thus: everywhere in the air, there weave and work the perfect forms of the essences of all speech-sounds, invisibly to earthly eyes. When we were children, they worked on our organisation until they built the larynx and speech organism, and then they more or less withdrew. Now they expect the human being to unite, with his own creative powers, the gifts he received freely, to become a creator of word and sound himself. This, however, he must consciously learn!

When the human being becomes capable of creating, in full consciousness, such a form that will *entirely match* the corresponding form in the objective form-world outside, at that moment this cosmic form will 'answer' him. It will become a 'mirror'; and, lighting up in the reflection-centre, it will shine towards him from without.

Just as the objective sound-world reveals itself to the human being through the reflected tone (as we showed in the reflection phase), so the objective word-world reveals itself through the reflected vowel. And the point from which it 'answers' him, as we said, lies in front of the mouth, *embedded in the same supersensible principle* of the human being in which the upper sound-pole is also anchored: *in the etheric body!*

This explains why we feel as though we were sucking in the vowels from the outside. Likewise it will be clear why they are divested of their heaviness.

In the end, because both factors — sound and word — are now *borne by the same supersensible principle*, they can appear again in a synthesis on a higher level.

* * * * *

What we might say in detail about the second factor of the speech-sound organism — about the nature of the consonants — can best be found in Rudolf Steiner's wonderful description in his lectures on speech formation. An attempt on our part to reproduce it in a shortened form would only impair the integrity of that presentation.

Hence we shall just go briefly into the treatment and transformation of the consonants as it relates directly to singing.

When one tries to grasp the essence of the consonants as we have done for the vowels in our work on their forms, one will experience the consonants very differently.

While the vessels of the vowels appear empty and hollow to the conscious forming-will, the consonants can only be experienced as 'filled activity'.

What was experienced as a permanent negative in the vessel-form of the vowel, is filled positively in the consonant form.

Whether one hisses with the S-sound, strikes with the T and K-sound, or vibrates with the R-sound, one is always filling in the form oneself. One is suddenly right in the midst of the air-activity, which — if one can apply this concept to the configuration of consonants — becomes a sort of form itself. To be sure, one will really be inside this 'action form' only *after* the *onset* of the consonant is past (be it the hissing onset on to F, V; striking on T, G, K; gently breathing on H, CH, or the whistling hiss on S, Z, etc.) Each time, this onset is experienced as a 'jump', as though one had to cross over a 'ditch', an 'abyss' — and this *experience* is actually the essential and characteristic one for the consonantal world. (Perhaps this can be felt most vividly when one makes a forceful 'implosion' on the consonants B, P, or K.)

Of course, this applies to the consonantal experience in singing, not in speech. In singing, however, this 'jump' makes a sudden interruption in the flow of the sound stream. With the exception of all the so-called liquids (M, N, L, etc.), which occupy a sort of middle position between consonant and vowel, the consonants are to a greater or lesser degree radical destroyers of the flowing sound element, while *rightly* formed vowels provide marvellous vessels for its manifestation.

When we have attained complete mastery of the vowel forms, and can now *hold on* consciously to their forms, which are in fact anchored into the very configuration of our muscles, then the jump across the abyss is transformed, becoming a *stride.*

When we step from one foot on to the other, we are really also 'jumping' over an abyss; only we do not notice it, because we have learned already as children to support ourselves on the standing foot until we have bridged the gap to the next step.

However, in order to really understand this question, it must be approached more *as a matter of consciousness* than of outward, physical-material activity.

To use this image once more: If, in jumping, one gauges too short in one's consciousness, the jump will also fall short, and one finds oneself in the ditch. In the same way in singing, one must learn with the help of one's inner

137

ear always to cast accurately in one's consciousness across from one vowel to the next, no matter how many and what kind of consonantal gaps open up inbetween. The consciousness, anchored and supported in the vessel-form of the vowels, will carry over any gap!

Thus it will be clear that the consonants can be practised only in conjunction with the vocalic forms, working on each and every combination.

Then, when we are ready to introduce into the sound stream such form-perfect vowels, which in turn can bridge the consonant-gaps, *then we have finally reached the aim of the schooling, then we will have attained true artistic singing.* This, however, involves a new consciousness for the true meaning of artistic text-singing.

Today, the artistic element in singing is thought to be more or less dependent on the singer's talent in conveying the *sense* or *content* of the text through the element of *feeling.* Here we may disregard the loudness or virtuosity of the singing voice. At this point, however, it becomes a real experience that what is truly artistic in singing must be sought elsewhere altogether. One will directly experience how language — as a spiritual entity — begins to manifest itself through the single sounds and syllables of speech, and how one is practically forced to perceive the artistic element in the *arising, moulding,* and *fading out* of the individual sounds and syllables.

In one's way of beginning the syllables and words and letting them end *with loving care,* in *consciously* allowing one word to come to an end, and equally consciously setting about the next word, while filling the space between with inner activity — *here alone is the true art in singing textual music;* for only in this way does one touch the creative element in speech directly. The artistic, creative element in the sound world, on the other hand, is reached

138

in liberating the tones from their bodily imprisonment. When we are in full possession of this consciousness, we will be able to experience a song as a being, on to whose sound-form we continually drape garments of different colours. To one who sings according to this school, with freed tones and weightless speech-sounds, the vowels are felt only as a means to endow the sound stream with characteristic colours. A hitherto unsuspected richness of colour combinations will stand at our command; we will colour the sound stream with them, so that in this respect we can really feel like an artist – like a painter in our own particular domain.

* * * * *

Through our discussion of the world of speech sounds we have arrived at certain special tasks. How can we realise them practically? We will be able to speak of this only in a most basic, schematic way, with a short survey of the different vowels in their mutual relationships.*

We have three groups of vowel-sounds. Within each of these three groups, the forms arise through closely related mouth, tongue, and lip positions – positions that flow one from the next. These three groups are:

1)   A, O, U,
2)   A, Ä, E, I,
3)   A, Ö, Ü.

When we sing the sequence A – O – U, and observe the movements which our speech-organism carries out, we

*For explanation of the vowel sounds and English 'equivalents'. See Translator's Note.

139

will notice that we close the oral cavity and lips in three stages. These movements remain within the same movement-tendency, only they become 'sharper'. Thus, the lip-opening is greater in A, but related in form to that in O; and U in turn is a narrowing and sharpening of O.

In the second sequence, the vowels A — Ä — E — I, the positions of the oral cavity and lips progress with a similar 'sharpening', only here not in a forwards direction, but laterally — breadthwise.

The third sequence is composed of the vowels A — Ö —Ü. Here again there are two stages of narrowing towards the front, but in a different manner than with A — O — U. Here, for example, the lower jaw and its muscles play a much greater role than with A — O — U, where chiefly the lips are responsible for the sharpening.

In the first and second sequences, one can actually distinguish four vowels as in the second, if one adds the two Scandinavian vowel-sounds U and Y. These actually come as natural continuations of the mouth-positions in sequences 1 and 3, like the I in the second sequence. So, taking account of the Swedish language as well, we would get the following little table:

1)   A, Å, O, U,
2)   A, Ä, E, I,
3)   A, Ö, Ü, Y.

When we practise singing each of these vowel-sequences, our ear will gradually learn to fix the right form and colour for each vowel *through its context in the sequence.*

And once again the circle is closed, so to speak: in the end, everything depends on the ear, on the ability to hear, to listen, to attend to the forming activity of the breath!

For this reason, it will be infinitely easier and simpler

for the student to grasp what we have written about the forming and colouring of the speech-sound world, if the teacher demonstrates everything live before him; then his *ear* is called upon as his main guide. For if only we have the opportunity to hear the forms correctly — even in a purely outward way, listening to another person sing them — then they unite creatively with the forces in our own breath, larynx and speech-organisation. In this way we slowly learn through imitation to form and mould them ourselves. The earlier such right forms are sung for us and can act on us, the easier this will be! If, for instance, we might experience only true, perfectly sung tones and word-forms in our childhood, then the whole of our later schooling would be child's play for us.

To be sure, one may not forget that this circumstance makes it necessary to be more careful than ever in judging the powers of each student, so that one does not demand too much hard work. The larynx is not really resilient until it is completely formed.

Very much, both general and specific, could still be said about the nature of these three vowel sequences — which in fact include all vowel-sounds. For example, one could show how each of these sequences can be experienced in direct relation to the threefold physiological make-up of the human being, itself a sort of reflection of the three soul-forces. Further, each of these three groups in itself can be looked at as an independent 'organic structure' with its own threefold relation to our singing organisation, manifested through its own particular quality.

Singing these three vocalic sequences one after another, with the attitude that one wishes them to show the direction they would like to go themselves as they are carried by the sound stream, one will notice that the first group A — O — U takes a purely horizontal direction. This straight

141

movement can be felt as a certain balance between above and below — the more so since it really represents a mean among these groups. For, the second sequence A — Ä — E — I shows an unmistakable tendency to move upwards, while the third group A — Ö — Ü — Y decidedly takes a downward direction.

Continuing to allow oneself to be directed by these speech-sound groups as one practises and observes, one will find that they also show their relation to the vibrating regions of the right vocal cord. The first group, A — O — U, which moves horizontally, will clearly reveal (if rightly sung) that it originates within the first and second vibratory centres of the vocal cord; for the essential nature of this group of vowels is directly expressed only in the sound-character produced by these two vibrating members together.

At another point we have shown that the two upper vibrating members, sounding together, form the sphere within which the *mezzoforte* incarnates, while the upper vibrating member by itself provides the basis for *piano* singing.

Thus, this first group can be felt as a sort of representative of the *dynamic mean.*

Attending now to the characteristic quality of the second group, A — Ä — E — I, one will quickly hear how this sequence of vowels, which flow upwards, has its home in the upper member of the right vocal cord; for only this sound-character matches the essential character of the second group. Similarly, we can recognise the third group, which vibrates downwards, as a representative of the *forte,* i.e. of the vocal cord vibrating as a whole.

It is as though the dynamics of singing itself were manifested through these three vowel-groups, in their essential natures and memberment.

It belongs to the most important and interesting discoveries one can make in the field of singing, when one realises that this very fact, with all of its consequences, actually represents the true basis for a *real culture* in singing. For, if one makes any attempt to give this fact its due, one will be forced to give up one's subjective bearing towards the will of the Musical; and one will be led to true listening, to objective attending. At the same time this inaugurates an attitude of soul which — if it is taught already in childhood — will raise one's consciousness of the true significance of singing (to which we will return later) to an entirely different level from the one which it unfortunately occupies in general today.

Moreover, this true listening will provide the foundation of a new gift for observation, a gift which can no longer be sought outside, or beyond, the subtle immaterial phenomena of singing.

From such an observation, one will quite rightly wonder how it is that these groups, which sound out of three different vibrating centres, can have the same first sound — A.

To this we must say something that would be much easier to understand by hearing it than in reading its description here:

The three different vibratory centres of our sound-organisation in fact each have an individual form of the vowel A, so that, strictly speaking, we must speak of three essentially different A-sounds. The A introducing the sequence Ä, E, I is completely different from the one beginning the group Ö, Ü, Y, and the A of the O, U group also is of a different nature. The difference in sound and form between these three A's is at least as great as, let us say, between an Ä and A sound, an O and U sound, etc.

A must simply be regarded as that speech-sound through

143

which the larynx proclaims itself; and since the larynx expresses its essentiality in three modes of sounding, it is not strange that it sounds through this basic speech-sound in different ways, depending on the vibratory centre(s) through which it manifests itself.

Hence, if we are looking for exercises by which we can learn to master the dynamics of singing (i.e. to move from *piano* to *forte* and back); we will best find them in conjunction with these three vowel-groups, since they represent the dynamics of singing itself. Furthermore, it is immediately evident that the best vowel to help us in this will be A, the basic vowel.

The aims of this book and its small framework do not permit us to go into greater detail on all these matters. This decision is also made on the grounds that all this is relatively easy to grasp through the living experience of hearing it oneself, while it must remain more or less theoretical and difficult to understand in such written descriptions.

So, if we wish to go on, and keep up the practical side of our presentation, we naturally come to the question as to the individual qualities and 'workings' of the chief organs which help in forming and perfecting the various sounds of speech: i.e., the question as to the physiology of the tongue, lips, etc., and also, particularly, the art of correct respiration.

Chapter Seven

THE PHYSIOLOGY OF THE TONGUE

The human tongue — how interesting it is in every respect, that mysterious organ which tirelessly and willingly works as our most immediate servant of the spirit of language! And how multifarious, how revealing is the knowledge one can win about correct singing, when one tries to observe this organ from a point of view more intimate than usual.

Both the outer form — with its incredible range of individual varieties — and especially the great panoply of movements it can perform, offer abundant material for a study — probably inexhaustible material.

If we were to write down everything there is to say on this subject, we would have another whole book. Therefore let the reader pardon the aphoristic nature of this description; for we must limit ourselves exclusively to that which is immediately connected with the rest of what we present here.

Let us look at the outer form of the tongue — that part of it which is visible in the mouth. We can recognise three areas of activity at first: the tip of the tongue, a middle, and a back part. This back part actually extends to the epiglottis — i.e. it extends down over the deep groove between the oral tongue and the epiglottis — and also connects the oral tongue with its invisible parts: the epiglottis and root or base of the tongue.

Further we can observe how early the tongue forms and develops its various shapes. Already in children, one can speak of several typical groups of tongue forms, some quite

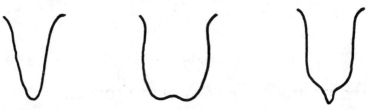

different from the others: we have, for example, one group in which the tongue is narrow, relatively thin, and has a well-defined tip. A second group displays a broad, rather limp, fleshy form without any definite tip, in exceptional cases (e.g. in one pathological child) actually curving inwards instead of coming to a tip. In a third group one can even find a very bizarre form in which the tip of the tongue looks as though it were tied off by a belt-like muscle which contracts around it. Then there are particularly long or short tongues, pale ones and red ones, smooth and rough, and so forth.

The contours of the middle and back portion of the tongue are usually hard to see, and they are not so important for us here as the surface of the tongue, with its almost chaotic network of lines and other irregularities: knots, depressions, etc.

First we shall look at the middle zone of the tongue. In almost all cases, there are numerous deep lines running through it, some along the length of it, others aslant and athwart. These lines are every bit as individual and various as those of the human hand. There are no two human beings whose tongues display the same lines.

Similarly, one can find the most curious irregularities. There are tongues, for instance, with deep hollows that will not unfold completely until the tongue is well stretched out. In any case, there is an almost inexhaustible variety of formations in this respect as well.

If one learns to understand the language of the lines and unevennesses, this knowledge can be very helpful in guiding the student. The 'reading' of this line-script, in conjunction with a consideration of the whole form and mobility of the tongue, will help to make a *sort of diagnosis* of the strengths and weaknesses in the student's singing-organisation.

To prevent possible misunderstanding, it must be emphasised that such 'reading' cannot in any way be compared with 'chirology' or 'palm-reading' and such-like practices. Rather, one must be acquainted with what spiritual science calls the 'physiological three-foldness of the human being' — for this is the only approach that can help one to understand fully what is intended here.

As the reader will remember, in the sound-direction phase we spoke of how one can relate each of the three regions of the right vocal cord to one of the three members of man's being. The same applies to the organ of the tongue. Dividing it into three 'members' or parts: the visible oral tongue, the epiglottis, and the root, we can see how these correspond in a certain way to the upper head-mental system, the middle rhythmic heart-lung-feeling system, and the lower limb-will system. However, just as the upper vibrating-member of the right vocal cord calls for its own division into three parts (which explains, for example, the origin of falsetto; see reflection phase), so we can also recognise a similar 'tripartition' in the oral tongue, relating to the way it moves and forms the sounds of speech. *Thus the oral tongue likewise refers us to the entire human being.*

If one turns one's attention to its physiology — to its snakelike mobility and almost unlimited capacity for forming the speech-sounds of countless linguistic idioms, then one will begin to appreciate what a complex organism the human tongue represents, and what wisdom is embodied in it.

147

In speaking and singing, every person is naturally highly dependent on the particular individual physiology of his or her tongue. If the tongue is sluggish or limp, relatively unresponsive to conscious control and therefore clumsy, this will be noticeable not only in the person's general manner of speech, but even in each single speech sound. This can be contrasted with a person whose tongue responds readily to the first impulse of speech, is well-penetrated by the consciousness and therefore willing and supple. One need only think of the speech of a drunken person. In accordance with his dimmed state of consciousness, he can only summon the activity of his tongue to babbling, semi-articulate sound-forms.

One might feel it would be enough to confront all these facts seriously in order to bring about a change. However, the attempt will soon show that there are fundamental causes at work, which lie anchored much deeper and faster than a good will alone could overcome. (Consider, for example, the almost insurmountable difficulties of the person who stutters or lisps.)

We touch one of the cardinal questions of this school when we become aware of the extremely close connection existing between the physical make-up of the tongue — as it has been formed from birth onwards in all its parts — and its capacity to react to the speech-command given by the human ego, i.e. to set all its muscles, small and large, in motion to form new sounds. The fact is that the relation of every single part of a muscle to the other muscles or parts of muscles, and to the whole of the organ, plays an enormous role. Where even one little muscle is unable to participate in forming a sound, this has the large consequence of *interrupting the continuity* of the formative force as it *tries to take effect*.

Nowadays it is the unfortunate fact, not only with

speakers and singers but with almost everyone, that there are a great number of such non-participating muscles remaining more or less motionless in the different zones of the tongue. This may seem a hard thing to say, but it does not take much effort to discover it in oneself. One only needs to begin working on the various speech-sounds energetically and attentively, repeating them over and over and always trying harder to include the *entire* speech organism, and one will soon start to sense the 'dead provinces'. (See preceding chapter.) One becomes aware that one cannot 'get at' this or that place with one's consciousness. *And this is the critical realisation: since the muscle cannot be reached with the consciousness, it remains inactive, 'dead'.*

A humorous little example of this can be seen in the first unsuccessful efforts of school children who — because their friends can already do it — absolutely must know how to wiggle their ears or scalps. (We have actually already given this example.) Through their persistent efforts they manage to probe with their consciousness in the direction of the muscle concerned, until one day it finally finds and penetrates it, thus taking control of it. The muscle is 'woken up', and they can wiggle their ears.

The situation is in fact quite similar with the muscles of our tongue, lips, palate, jaws, etc. We cannot reach them with our consciousness, for it does not know the way. *So they remain shut off.*

Here it is a wonder to observe with what wisdom the genius of language works within us; for it calls on other muscles, not originally intended for this activity, to fill in the 'gaps' as best they can and replace the non-functional muscles. (In the preceding chapters we have touched on this theme several times.) However, the natural result of this is the speech-forms arising are not pure and true, but broken and distorted.

149

To choose some crude examples: When the speaker does not have command over the very tip of the tongue, he will say instead of a true, hissing S-sound a lisped one, in which the tip of the tongue is pushed through between the upper and lower teeth; instead of an R trilled with the tip of the tongue, he will produce a so-called velar R with the back of the tongue; instead of a light L welling up in front, a thick velar L such as Americans sometimes use in speaking an unaccustomed language. Here the tongue, instead of pressing against the upper front teeth, wanders back to the upper palate.

These examples should suffice to give a notion of what we mean. It goes without saying that there are hundreds of intermediate degrees and gradual deviations from the perfectly formed speech-sounds.

It will be our task, however, to apply all our resources to seek out these excluded muscles and bring them correctly within the sphere of our consciousness.

But what is the ideal form of the tongue?

A well-formed tongue of a really healthy human being bears a certain resemblance to a plant leaf, e.g. to a large sorrel leaf. It has a slim but firm form, coming to a nice, not-too-sharp rounding in front. Like the leaf, down the very middle it has a groove or line running its whole length; and this is sometimes even double, so that the tiny strip of tongue between the two lines appears thickened, giving it the appearance of the central vein of a leaf. As on the leaf, many littler lines run out of it on both sides, but never causing depressions or distortions, especially not disturbing the straightness of the midline. A midline deformed into a zigzag, or even running back into itself and disappearing, indicates that the middle and back part of the oral tongue is not properly developed, but lax, powerless, sluggish, and inaccessible to the consciousness. Then one can be sure that there are many small muscles and muscle groups there which are remaining still, unable to participate in forming various speech-sounds. Then, because other muscles come in to help, connections run criss-cross, which leads to slight cramping and finally manifests itself outwardly in the jagged lines, hollows, and other unevennesses.

In little babies, as well as in children as late as the ninth or tenth year, one can see that the middle and back portions of the oral tongue always take part in a definite and energetic way. Strangely, it is often these very portions of the tongue which are quite limp and dead in professional singers, not to speak of singers who have 'sung themselves out'.

Who has not observed how, in a screaming infant, the whole tongue from the tip to the very back — sometimes even showing the epiglottis — is stretched so tightly, so energetically, that it begins to tremble? And the delicate, smooth form of such a little tongue — is it not really similar to a rose petal?

However, as the child begins to develop his intelligence and approaches puberty, a slow change comes about in the back part of the oral tongue and, especially, in the epiglottis. While in the baby the whole tongue still functions as *one*, now there comes a sort of dissociation between the tip and middle of the tongue, on the one hand, and the back part of the oral tongue, the epiglottis, and the root of the tongue on the other hand.

This alteration, which is connected with a shift in consciousness and soul-life in the child, is not only in the functioning of the tongue, but penetrates in a real way into its physical make-up, and slowly, a slackening, paralysis, or also hardening spreads over the back part of the tongue and the epiglottis. The result is that the muscles located in the groove between the epiglottis and the back

151

part of the tongue no longer have the power to maintain the epiglottis in its former upright position; hence it slowly collapses, leaning backwards — or to the side according to the individual constitution — towards the root of the tongue. At the same time one can notice a clear decrease (one could also call it a coarsening) in the ability of these parts to meet the intentions of the formative will of the speech organism; the back part of the oral tongue becomes ever more sluggish and unwieldy, not only cutting itself off from the movements of the other parts of the tongue, but also radiating a paralysing influence into the middle of the tongue.

The immediate result of this is that we experience not only a loss of our ability to form really pure vowel forms, but that we likewise lose a consciousness of how these vowels should properly sound. For the centre of the tongue is the chief area for the forming of vowel sounds, while the tip and, in part, the back zone of the tongue are involved more in the consonantal element: d, t, r, s, l and g, k, h, ch (See translator's note). Certainly, fully formed vowels extend both to the tip and to the back part of the tongue, calling on the activity of the whole tongue; nevertheless, the *heart* of all vowels, the point from which the moulding activity arises, can be sought only in the middle part of the tongue.

This is why, of all the vowels, I is lost first; because this vowel can only be formed rightly when the *centre* of the tongue, *in its full breadth*, is pressed up against the palate so as to create a cross-line, through which the true, closed form of the I-vowel can sound.

With a slackening such as we have described, it is obvious that the middle of the tongue can no longer accomplish this activity, so that we must make do with all kinds of pseudo-I-forms and distortions.

Listen very attentively to the I of a musical, two to three-year-old child, when it is singing just for itself, at bedtime for example, or for its doll. What one can learn from this is more convincing, and can tell us more than any description, no matter how clever.

The situation with the other vowel forms is not much better, especially when they involve strong lip-forms as well as these tongue-forms, as in a true U, Ü, Ö, or Y. In these cases, the formative will really feels 'homeless'; it can only swing back and forth between the meagre possibilities still available to it, only to give up in the face of the insuperable difficulties.

And this brings us the opportunity, for the first time, to refer to something which one cannot take too seriously, for it must be counted as part of the very basis of this school:

Up to now, though we have often spoken of the difference between the speech and sound organism, we have not dealt with common boundaries of their spatial domains. Naturally there is a boundary, a boundary-organ defining and separating these two organisations, and this is the *epiglottis. The epiglottis serves as the back partition, wall, or 'gate-keeper'* (whatever one wishes to call it) *of the speech organism*, against the *sound stream flowing behind it*. But it can only do this so long as it maintains its natural, healthy uprightness, which enables it to form a real closure.

If we make use of the image of a vessel again, then we may say that for the speech-forms, a collapsed epiglottis is like a hole broken out of the back wall of a vessel.

So long, however, as this 'boundary post' can function properly, the singer does not come into danger of losing himself onesidedly in the sound element; this danger only appears when the 'border guard' begins to become lax and limp, falling down. Then this 'checkpoint' no longer operates at the border, and our consciousness gradually loses the ability to orient itself properly as to whether we stay within the permitted limits in forming the speech-sounds, or go beyond them into the sound area. *Our consciousness loses grasp of the difference between sound and speech-activity*. However, as we have already shown, this means nothing less than our total delivery into the hands of the forces of decadence.

To be sure, this process of downward development proceeds slowly, almost unnoticeably for the young person — but hence all the more relentlessly. And when the moment in development comes where the childhood forces — which up to now have let the child instinctively do what is correct — must begin their retreat, unless they are *replaced* by proper instruction in singing and speaking (in which the teacher *demonstrates before the pupils*), then the feared degeneration simply creeps on unimpeded. After the twenty-fifth year it can scarcely be checked; for a voice which has been ruined during its period of change cannot be fully repaired. This applies equally for boys and girls.

When one considers this state of affairs, and realises that all young people now training their voices for professional purposes have gone this path of sorrows, even if unconsciously (and in addition we must think of all the damage inflicted on the larynx itself), then one can begin to grasp the whole tragedy of their situation, with all its disappointed hopes and expectations.

One will also be able to understand a statement which Rudolf Steiner once made in relation to this school: If, through this kind of singing, one can help the young person over the delicate transition of puberty, it will mean that he will keep his youthfulness much longer.

Truly, how could they be helped by the generally current form of singing pedagogy, which knows nothing of these injuries and their origins? Only spiritual science – and, in the rarest cases, observed personal experience – is capable of explaining these things.

From what has been said, it will be clear that a school of singing which wishes to be worthy of the name in our times must dedicate its first and most earnest efforts precisely to the *correction of these injuries*. Our consciousness must be enabled to enter these abandoned provinces again; and we will achieve this by concentrating our consciousness intensely on the formative power of the breath, and by consciously attending to the perfect models of the speech-sounds which we can hear within us.

Through such quite conscious work on our own tongue, it can be *transformed back into a unified organ*, as it was in babyhood and the first seven years of life. The *entire tongue* – the oral tongue, epiglottis, and root of the tongue – must in the right way be made capable again of participating *wholly* in the forming of each sound of speech. This happens in the following way: the middle of the tongue must have an enlivening effect on the back part of the tongue, the latter must give back to the epiglottis its lost power to stay erect, and from here the enlivening, regenerating power will flow of itself to the root of the tongue, including the hyoid bone.

In order to treat this subject thoroughly, it would really be necessary to go into the physiology of the other parts of our speech-forming organism – the lips, jaws, corners of the nose, palate, etc.; for all of these muscular provinces work in most intimate connection with the tongue. On each of these groups one could write a little book; for each province is a little world in itself, and moreover all of them have close interconnections – in fact, in singing they are partially dependent on one another. Thus, the activity of the upper lip is closely linked with the activity of the

155

muscles of the upper back palate, the corners of the nose with the muscles of the vocal cords, the musculature of the lower lip and also lower jaw with the epiglottis and root of the tongue, the corners of the mouth with the muscles of the throat walls, etc. Some of these connections are not obvious at first; yet each of them could be thoroughly substantiated with examples.

If one has a knowledge of these connections which one is able to use in a practical way, this will be a tremendous help for the student. For naturally, these muscle groups as well must be mastered, singly and together, so that they can be incorporated as willing servants into the singing-organism.

* * * * *

When one surveys all the tasks and difficulties we have presented — unfortunately only in their rough outlines — it may seem that the young person would be disheartened in the face of them. The efforts appear to extend infinitely, and the demands on one's patience, endurance, and faith grow to almost unimaginable dimensions. Who should feel this more honestly and plainly than we ourselves! For we have put this path behind us — under the most un-favourable and tough conditions thinkable — and we know well enough these battles, pains and disappointments, but also purest joys and inner blessing, out of our own experience.

One may not forget that it is a different thing when one masters the several stages step by step, *growing oneself* in the course of a long period of schooling, than when one *reads* a report which collects in a moment all the difficulties together, yet must leave out the most important thing: *the organic growth and becoming.*

156

Whoever loses sight of this may well lose the courage to fight against these damages and transformations of his organisation, and turn away from this genuinely hard — more than hard — work. We have the deepest understanding for such a decision; for we are thoroughly aware that the difficulties in overcoming those hindrances in uncovering the voice are extraordinarily great. In our conviction, this is owing to the far-reaching degeneration to which the physical speech and singing organisation is subject in many adults today. Although we believe and have always found through experience that these organic difficulties and obstacles can be overcome — with a good will and consistent practice, as well as patience and persistence — still there can be cases in which the student's strength does not measure up to these difficulties.

It would be a fatal error to think that the school and the aims it sets are responsible for this failure. The fact that hard struggles often must occur is actually inherent in the nature of the school; however, this struggle can only be seen as a positive means of protection and help against the decay of our singing-organisations today. Certainly these difficulties will occur less when a right form of singing-education forestalls the loss of the child's healthy vocal capacities, and the suppleness of the child's organisation remains.

In this regard, we can best characterise our school thus: *It is a declaration of war for the maintenance, restoration, and healing of the 'instruments'* built into the human body as the sole means by which the art of song and word can come to manifestation.

If we all had enjoyed a correct singing pedagogy and speech formation in school from our seventh year onwards, these would have *caught* and *worked against* the arising of this damage, and we would have very little of such 'hard

157

work' indeed in our later education in singing. The truth of these words has shown itself more than once in actual life!

However, when people who suffered particularly heavily under these degenerative processes and who throughout their schooling were driven to plunder further their organic forces through screaming and a lack of any real culture in singing (not to speak of the consequences brought on by a wrong form of singing teaching) — when such people find the resistance of inoperative organs impossible to overcome who can be amazed? Nor is it remarkable when these unfortunates finally seek to escape from their difficulties by *excluding the speech organism as much as possible,* taking refuge in the sound-experience. Then they search desperately in the domain of sound for some method which will help them to master the speech-world. That is, they take the lawful elements of *instrumental music* and attempt to apply them to singing. (Through the use of flowing melody, rhythm, beat, by being relaxed, etc.)

Whenever one ignores the laws inherent and proper to the word, regarding it as a disagreeable but unavoidable 'attachment' and allowing it to appear just as it is, untransformed, one is really disregarding the existence of the word-organism. And certainly it is possible to produce tones according to the laws of purely instrumental music, but can this be called *singing*? True singing exists only in a balanced cooperation of the arts of tone and word. Another name would have to be found for that one-sided kind of vocalising.

To be sure, one *can* 'sing' in such a way. The only question is how long the instrument — the throat — can bear it. One often forgets that it makes a vast difference whether the instrument is oneself or if it is an external musical instrument with quite a different level of stability and endurance than the human throat.

For musical song we have only this one delicate instrument, which is built into our physical body. And if we do not say 'yes' to the work on our physical body, this really means that we simply have *no interest in the reconstruction and perfection of our instrument.*

Of course it is much more comfortable to leave the body as it has grown. For our egoism it is more natural to revel in the satisfying experience of swelling sound than to descend, as it were, to our unwieldy hardened organism and work to bring it up with us and redeem it.

However, if we call up the power of renunciation, we will eventually make the muscular 'material' of all provinces of our speech-organisation permeable again, so that it will obey the formative will (so far as our individual material permits this). Then we will be able to mould pure speech-forms; and furthermore, we will acquire the capacity to magnify and widen these forms in such a way that we can bring them to the reflection centre of the word. With these speech-forms we shall give birth to words which we can be inside of with our *whole* being.

* * * * *

And now to the practical side of this work. The necessity of enlivening and making our tongue mobile must have become clear to some teachers of singing, at least in principle. In any case, here and there one meets attempts to understand these important questions. Unfortunately, such attempts, even when they seek for practical means of help, tend to come more out of intellectual good will than out of living involvement with these facts. Thus, in order to enliven the back part of the tongue, one simply presses it down with a rather large spoon and let the student always sing thus. And the tongue does assume a more correct

159

position during this treatment; but when the spoon is taken away, one is back where one started.

If, despite our will, the tongue refuses to follow the impulse to the right speech-form and go down out of its *own* mobility, then the use of a foreign object will scarcely achieve very much. Furthermore, such a procedure works directly with the anatomy of the tongue, and thus directs our consciousness at the organic level.

There are also methods, taken quite seriously, by which the tongue is made more elastic and mobile through a special kind of mechanical gymnastics: for example, the tongue must lick the lips in the prescribed manner from left to right, from right to left; it must be made 'thick' or 'thin', etc.

How can one believe that one will accomplish anything towards reforming the middle and back parts of the tongue and the epiglottis, by assigning the *tip of the tongue* a half or a whole hour of 'movement lessons'; it already serves us for many hours a day in speaking, and mostly through the tireless movement of its tip! Most of these exercises are tailored for the tip of the tongue, no matter how clever or complex they are. And once more, this is a procedure which, because it is not linked with simultaneous singing, brings our consciousness into direct connection with the organic level.

If a certain exertion were at least asked of the tongue — for example, to stretch out energetically and touch the tip of the nose or chin — then at least part of the posterior mass of the tongue would be shaken out of its phlegmatic rest into wholesome activity.

Around forty years ago, there was an ingenious Swedish singing teacher who made her students sing with outstretched tongues, which they had to hold by a handkerchief wrapped around the tip — and she accomplished really good progress.

160

But in the way of which we have been speaking, one cannot reach the formative forces of the tongue in a really fruitful manner, as one soon realises.

The tip of the tongue is so lively and mobile that, so long as it is allowed to move freely and unhindered, it pushes itself into the foreground; then the far weaker, sluggish movements of the other parts of the tongue hardly come into play, let alone being strengthened or participating again.

If we wish to reach the back parts of the tongue, including the epiglottis, in a way suited to our purposes, then we must seek for ways to first shut out the snakelike mobility of the tip. Only in this way can we bring the back parts of the tongue and the epiglottis into stronger participation. If, for example, the tip is held fast by pressing it firmly against the gums of the lower front teeth and keeping it there, then one is no longer in a position to form a speech-sound *normally*. That is, the tongue can no longer move normally as a *whole*, and so the formative will must turn to the back parts and form the speech-forms out of *these alone*. This forces these parts into activities and movements which are 'abnormal' for them, but which they are quite capable of performing.

And to develop these latent capacities is our aim! With this or a similar way of exercising, these parts of the tongue can be made so elastic, so reactive and willing that finally they will assume of their own power the position which could at first be attained only by pressing with a spoon. And before one has achieved this, one will never be able to form correct, perfectly round forms for the speech sounds. Thus, a pure O or A sound can never be achieved without this lowering of the middle and back part of the tongue.

In fact this is only *one* of the measures we can use. In

161

correct attempts to awaken the back parts and the epiglottis, it is important to give the tongue such tension that the stretching reaches right down to the root of the tongue and the tongue-bone, encompassing the entire tongue. This can be accomplished by gradually pushing the tip of the tongue *under itself* more and more, as far down and back as it can be bent. One does this while practising, and at the same time one keeps a sharp watch for whatever the speech-forming entity is trying to do with the entire organ of the tongue.

Very interesting observations can be made in this. The first time students are asked to adopt this position, it often happens that they cannot figure out which way to push the tip of the tongue. Instead of going down, it frequently moves along the upper palate, wanders to either side, or remains still, undecided, in the middle — not to mention the case (a unique one) where despite all good will, the tongue past by the teeth every time, and landed in the space between the teeth and lip.

On the other hand, when one observes how adroitly children set about it when they want to learn to whistle or do other contortions with their tongue, this is an outer sign and picture of what we have said.

Certainly this unwonted stretching of the tongue sometimes causes an uncomfortable feeling — it can even bring about mild (and quickly passing) cramps — nevertheless one soon notices how the tongue begins to meet the formative will more and more, how the dead provinces awaken, and how the epiglottis regains its power of uprightness.

Here we can only mention that there are many more and quite different exercises, among them certain ones relating to the above-mentioned interconnections between muscular regions. These exercises also help considerably in achieving this task.

Such tongue exercises come in already in the beginning of the schooling, at the same time as the sound-directing exercises with NG. One must learn to see them as one of the most basic elements of the schooling; however, *any* such exercise of the tongue *must be accompanied by simultaneous singing.*

It cannot be repeated too many times: conscious, systematic work on the organic level will never go un-punished unless a tone is sung at the same time. Even a *spoken* tone is not enough to protect us in such work. For only in singing does the sound stream come into play; and it is in the sound stream that a power lies which can compensate and protect against the consequences of direct manipulation on the organic level. And this is also why such work is only possible in learning to sing, but not in correct speech formation.

Consonants as well as vowels should be practised intensively in this tongue position. In fact, besides dealing in this way with the individual speech sounds, one also takes whole songs, trying to maintain a clear pronunciation of all sounds while keeping the tongue motionless in this position, and in addition biting the molars firmly against each other.

This is strenuous work; but when one has developed a certain technique in this 'bound singing', the moment one releases all the bonds and restrictions one will be surprised how great the blessing is which this method brings.

It should not be too hard to see that a tongue 'trained' thus, when it is later left to itself (naturally one should not have to think of one's tongue in finished singing), will be capable of much greater mobility, elasticity, and willingness than without such 'training'.

* * * * *

Having seen that such training of the tongue is necessary and important so that we can make full and conscious use of its formative forces, now we must look at the same necessity from another, no less significant, point of view. Here we touch on a connection which in its real significance has been totally forgotten by today's singing teaching: the highly intimate relations existing between the activity of the posterior zones of the tongue and the *respiration* in singing.

In a way, these two factors are 'allies' — complementary opponents against correct singing: the respiratory process plays more the role of active, the sluggish tongue that of passive opponent. They are so closely related in their activities that one might speak of a dependence between them. Thus, if one simply gives it sufficient attention, one will experience how a particularly lethargic, unformed back half of the tongue brings with it a bad, impeded kind of respiration, while improper respiration has a paralysing effect on the epiglottis and root of the tongue. Hence it is not only of great importance for the tongue itself that we work it over thoroughly: in the process we are doing something of infinite importance towards freeing and regulating the whole breathing process.

From the viewpoint of anatomy and physiology as well, this relationship is not hard to confirm. One need only think of the role played by the epiglottis in undisturbed breathing: it has the task of closing off the windpipe while we swallow, so that nothing gets in it. Thus the epiglottis and the whole root of the tongue stand in the closest contact with the breath-stream. If they become limp and sluggish, they collapse, *narrowing* the 'channel' of the breath. When the epiglottis has lost some of its uprightness, it also gets in the way of the breath-stream. Without fail, this must impair the process of respiration. When the epiglottis regains its uprightness and full elasticity, this has a tremendous importance for the entire breathing process, which we shall now consider in some detail.

Chapter Eight

THE ART OF BREATHING

Correct respiration is an art in itself!
Which singer has not experienced the human breathing-process as a more or less independent entity which, sometimes growing into a monster, confronts him demanding to be 'tamed' and guided? And how often one must admit to oneself in all honesty that one cannot do it, that one feels oneself at the mercy of this most mysterious activity of the human organism. In despair one seeks for ways which will open a deeper understanding of the laws at work, so that one will at least have some foothold from which to work towards effortless, well-established˙ respiration in singing.

However, since this search generally springs more from the good will of the intellect, and not so much from an intimate sensitivity to the immediate phenomena and interconnections of the respiratory process, both in singing and in daily life, despite all our efforts it leads us into chaos with giant steps!

For in our times almost every method of singing has created its own doctrine of breathing, with exercises based on it, which it propagates and employs without further ado.

It is true, this is an age when most people will believe only in things which they can grasp with their minds, when only material things seem to be real; and so perhaps it is understandable that singing teaching as well has tried to make sense of the respiration process in the same terms. For from this point of view, teachers and artists have no choice left but to construct some kind of breathing method by way of pure theory, either on a mechanical analogy, or out of a sum of single scientific facts.

When, however, one turns towards these problems and their various solutions equipped with the living experience attained through our school for uncovering the voice, one sees clearly how little all these searchers know about the true nature of breathing — not only regarding singing, but of the fundamental concept of breathing in itself.

If one has had the good fortune to enter more deeply into these mysteries by means of spiritual science, one will have to come to a disquieting realisation: in every respect we have gone so far from the right way of understanding and mastering this process that we will not find it again unless we summon up a will to reverse our direction completely and break through to new conceptions which match the reality of its true nature.

It is undoubtedly difficult to come to a clear idea of 'natural' breathing (i.e. breathing removed from our volition, breathing in itself), because in many people of our day this process is in a pathological, decadent state. And this fact explains why science has not been able to arrive at unequivocal insights on the breathing process.

In earlier times things were different. Then, a knowledge of correct breathing — in art as well — was simply a natural part of human *consciousness*. Today this *consciousness* has been lost, and into the empty space the intellect has entered as a searching factor.

The reign of this arch-enemy of all true art has wrought so much damage in the domain of respiration since those former times that a whole book would be needed to describe it conscientiously. But once again, it must suffice us only to touch on the most basic issues, whether negative or positive.

167

Thus, much has been written in our times about the ancient mystery schools; and whoever is acquainted with what is known as yoga, the occult school of the Orient, knows that *consciously trained* breathing was an essential element in it.

It is the opinion of many today that by going back to such ancient exercises, to which we can of course gain only a second-hand, purely theoretical relation, something could be done towards correcting this degeneration.

But this is most definitely not the case! What was right for those ancient times cannot serve us, because since then the basic conditions of mankind have changed completely. We live in a time when we actually *should know nothing* of the breathing process and all its consequences; if it is to be healthy and normal, it must flow in *unconsciousness.* For someone from the West, it should seem absurd to speak of breathing exercises in the same sense as sport or other training exercises. The entire domain of breathing has been withdrawn from human volition since those ancient times; and now it is subject to quite other laws. Who has not experienced how it is no longer *possible* to breath naturally when one directs one's attention to the breathing process?

Yet how this fundamental law is sinned against! *Terrible damage is caused* just by treating the breath on analogy to something mechanical! Exercises are created at will, and used without the accompaniment of a sung tone to support them: the *breath itself* is made the object of observation and exercise. The intellect, however, does not immediately perceive this damage, because the connections of cause and effect usually are separated in time, thus escaping external observation.

It is simply a fact: one cannot with impunity manipulate the respiration process at will. If, without singing, one makes the breath the object of observation and exercise, in reality one gives oneself over to physiological processes which take place within the body. The inevitable effect of this is that one is bound more closely and tightly to one's physical body. Such a more intimate connection calls forth organic changes; but since these do not appear for some time, it is not easy for the ordinary consciousness to recognise their origin.

Such damage can manifest itself in a great number of ways. In more favourable cases, the singing-organisation slowly· but steadily hardens — both the sound organisation (larynx, ear, etc.) and the speech organs (tongue, epiglottis, etc.) — until singing becomes a labour of Sisyphus, and the end has come for the singer.

On the other hand, the consequence can also be serious illnesses whose cause is as yet unknown to medical science.

In contrast, when breathing exercises are used in conjunction with *properly sung* tones, then the *tone-experience* pushes to the foreground of our consciousness. This is an extra-physical experience; and when one concentrates on something outside or above the physical, one raises oneself out of the material level. This results not in a consolidation, but a loosening — the exact opposite — and this in turn affects the two singing organisations, giving them a greater flexibility, and thus also enhancing their ability to react.

In fact there *is* something for us to learn from those ancient traditions, and that is the *creative,* life-giving power of the breath. Once we have become fully conscious of this (as we have described in chapter 6), it will not be hard to understand that the question of correct or incorrect breathing takes on a tremendous importance, particularly in such a school as our school for uncovering the voice.

Although singing teachers speak often enough of 'right' or 'wrong' breathing, in general they have only a vague notion that much — *very* much — of the blame for bad singing today must be ascribed to a wrong way of breathing. For most of them it is still a secret that in truth, both for the art of song as well as that of speech, *more depends* on right breathing than on *all other factors.* Hence one can understand why they deal with this factor in the way we have described.

In that form of pedagogy, air is usually thought of quantitatively: one needs as *much air* as possible in order to 'form' the tones, to 'hold' them for a long time, and especially to 'prop them up' (there are many such expressions). So their main aim is to train the respiratory organs (chest and lungs) to expand as far as possible during inhalation. This quantity of air is then amassed into an 'air column', and this is laid as a material foundation under the tone, so that it is well 'founded', etc. Costal breathing is most often recommended, because it brings about the greatest extension of the chest and lungs.

Through all we have just said, one should be able to sense that this attitude cannot be brought into harmony with the laws of true singing. If the tone is to become the objective tone, as we have described, then it must flow down through the organism effortlessly, filled with sound. And this totally excludes the possibility that it could be *supported by anything organic in the human being,* even just a materially conceived 'air column'. For this is an approach which has caused the chief confusions in this area.

No, for a true understanding of the respiration process, it is essential to grasp that in the activity of singing it should not be anything more special for us than it is in our usual everyday activities — eating, playing, speaking, etc. In other words:

As little as the respiration process should be noticed in

170

all ordinary daily activities of a healthy human being, just as little should it disturb us in singing.

However, to understand this fully, we must come to a *new*, truthful view of the essential nature of this process of breathing. More exactly, we must gain knowledge of *how it operates in our time.*

This depends solely on our ability to penetrate to the very fundaments of this process and to evaluate and 'read' its physiological aspects correctly.

What is true of science is just as true for art: thousands, even millions, pass by some natural phenomenon without grasping its secret. Only one who has the gift for penetrating observation — one might say, a wisdom in sensing facts — will be able to uncover the general laws underlying the phenomena (e.g. Galileo and the swinging church lamp of Pisa).

It is true that thinking must enter in as well; still, the art of concentrated observation is its original stimulus, and will also be the decisive factor. The fact that some interested persons 'observe' the respiratory process does not say much. One will only come to decisive findings when one is able to study it without any preconceptions and prejudices, whether old or new, personal or general, and quite independently of any hindrances or accompanying phenomena. And this, as we have said, is a rather difficult task to perform. Because all human beings breathe differently, and most of them badly, it is not easy to distinguish between decadent phenomena and the undisturbed 'healthy' physiology of breathing.

Thus once again we find ourselves forced to say something which must be extremely hard for many readers to understand, and may seem quite bizarre; yet it is essential, for *this very* insight is in fact the new foundation for everything of importance we wish to present here.

171

Let us first put this question: What role is played by the element of the air in relation to the sound element, the tone? Is it really so, as many people see it, that we form the tone from the air? And even if we upset all views on this subject, both scientific and lay, we must answer this question with a decisive no.

Air — the breath — fulfills quite another function in relation to the sound stream, the tone. It gives it a kind of living, flowing yet resistant medium, so that the sensibly inaudible tone can enter the realm of the audible.

Rudolf Steiner once used this image: As man stands on the earth, so the tone stands on the *flowing element of the air.* Just as man could not be there without the earth beneath his feet, so the tone would 'fall through' if the air stream did not prevent it from continuing to move in the *inaudible* realm. In order to stand on the earth, we do not need to create ourselves each time out of earth again; no more do we create or form the tone out of air each time.

The tone has actual being; it exists of itself. The flowing stream of the air is the element which carries it and makes it audible.

Here the emphasis belongs on the word 'flowing'; for it is the *movement* of the air which is of importance. It is through our ability to *move* air in ourselves that we can sing — in fact, that we can live at all. In breathing what we really need is not the air in itself, but the movement of the air.

In singing as well, it is the moving of the air that matters, *not* as present-day singing teaching believes, the amount of air we breathe in and out — air which we then gather into a more or less motionless, compact 'supporting column'!

We should remember that we are far from breathing just with the lungs: we breathe with the entire surface of our skin as well! But because *this* part of the respiratory process is *radically* removed from our consciousness, we forget — at least in our practical attitude towards the respiratory process — to include in our reckoning this far greater air activity at all. In any case, consciously applied breathing techniques today take account only of the air breathed in through the lungs. And yet for singing, this very air which streams in and out through the epidermis is at least as important as the lung air-stream. A reflected tone, which sounds as though the space around the human being were sounding — the objective tone, in other words — would not be able to become manifest if it were not borne along and made audible by this air-stream as well, which flows un-noticed, in, out, and all around the human being.

Obviously we cannot dispense with the lung air-stream! But we ought not to forget that it represents only *one part* of the whole process; and above all we must be clear that it may not be subject to any principle but the whole process itself, which is governed by the basic principle of *movement* or rhythm — in fact, it *is* rhythm. *The fact that the lung-breathing process has fallen out of the whole process of respiration* has led to the degeneration we have spoken of. More precisely, the lung breathing-process has *fallen out of the unified rhythm* of the whole process. Today it leads a more or less independent existence as an estranged part of the whole, because we have forced (both voluntarily and involuntarily) other rhythms on to it, formed out of our individual difficulties.

From this it follows that our task must be to *join the lung breathing-process into the whole process of respiration again*. That is, we must strive consciously to bring lung-breathing into the *unified* rhythm of the *whole* respiratory process, by working with the air in the right way.

Now if the breathing process may not penetrate into consciousness, as we have shown, nevertheless it will be understandable that in order to retrain it we are forced to deal consciously with it *for a time;* only the important question is: How?

In artistic performance, any previous training must be 'forgotten'. So, if one has become habituated to a false mode of respiration, ways and means must be found by which one can wean oneself from it and acquire the correct one.

How is this to be done? We will achieve this correct mode of respiration when we succeed in *strengthening* the unified rhythm of the breathing process by means of appropriate movements. Little by little, the total process will attain the strength to draw the lung breathing-process back into its original rhythm, incorporating it into the whole.

To execute movements, however, we need the help of our muscular system. Hence, for this task we must look for the muscles which serve us in making these rhythmic movements, so that we can strengthen them and bring them to life.

If we could learn to stop clinging to the air itself (as when we try to take in as much air, quantitatively, as we can), and let the breathing process itself determine the amount of air it needs, then we would already have taken a big step towards our goal and would not have to go any more roundabout ways. However, a great deal of experience has shown that we cannot accomplish this without auxiliary means.

It is the rhythmic element that has proved the most helpful. We should do breathing exercises thus: in singing, we must *set in motion* specific muscles which play a primary role in the physiology of breathing, and which will have a direct influence on in- and exhalation; and their movements should have a definite rhythmic character.

While doing this, we should let the experience of these rhythmic movements come to the foreground of our consciousness, concentrating completely on their rhythm. In other words, to approach the breathing process in singing, we must 'clothe' it in rhythmic movements! In this way our consciousness is turned away from the breathing, and the question of the quantity of air used recedes into the background by itself.

The 'outer' air which we breathe in can be experienced in a certain way as 'dead' matter. But when we take it into ourselves and set it in motion, it changes; like everything we 'incorporate', it becomes alive.

Continually permeating 'dead' matter with life, passing it through ourselves, and giving it out again — *in this activity we experience the true being of the breathing process. Only through this principle* can we learn to really understand and guide the respiratory process.

Thus, when we do away with breathing exercises relating to the greatest possible intake of air, and turn our activity, while singing, towards those muscles primarily related to breathing movements (which muscles these are, we will see directly), *energising* and making them *supple* by linking their activity with the rhythm, then the respiratory processes will gradually recede out of our consciousness. And finally, we will experience the real fulfilment of this requirement: the breathing process should disturb us as little in singing as in all other daily occupations.

Then one also knows that this fear of not having enough air, this convulsive clinging to the material air, is the crudest enemy of a correct respiration process.

If, on the other hand, one experiences breathing as a *movement process* in the air, then an independence of the breathing process from the process of singing comes about of itself. In fact, one reaches the point where it makes no difference whether one makes use of the movements in breathing the air in, or in breathing it out.

Of course, there are many other capacities which play a large role here, only some of which have been mentioned in the preceding chapters; and these must still be acquired!

Thus, if the epiglottis hangs limp, putting a 'stumbling block' in the path of the breath, then the *continuity of the air flow is disturbed*. Or if those parts of the human organism which carry out the rhythmic movements during in- and out-breathing do not function properly, either because they are too flabby or too hard, this will have a critical effect on the entire process. Thus we must see to it that these muscles are activated, 'incorporated' into the consciousness — and hence into the living process — once again.

And this brings us to the practical side of our work on the breathing process.

First of all we must answer this question: Where do the unified movements of the breathing process originate, and which muscles of the human body directly serve the respiratory process?

The unified, healthy, and proper movement of the breathing process begins in the *region of the solar plexus,* which has a very close functional connection with the musculature of the diaphragm. Hence it is only these muscles which concern us, as well as the abdominal muscles, which as bearers of movement are intimately connected with the diaphragmatic muscles.

Now if we try objectively to observe what happens in so-called costal breathing, we see that the proper point of origin of the movement is displaced into the area of the lungs themselves, or to the extension-movements of the chest and lungs.

So here we have the root of the evil! By dealing with the breathing process with a view towards quantitative air-intake, we create *new centres set apart* from the normal, healthy, unified process which should stream through the whole person! And as though this were not enough, we dam up the air stream and hold it motionless in these foreign centres; and then we wonder that we cannot find harmonious, self-established respiration in singing.

It is true that part of the responsibility for these difficulties must be placed on the general state of development of contemporary mankind. For like the tongue, at a certain age the breathing process undergoes a change, a hardening and coarsening. And as with the tongue, the *unity of the process falls apart,* so that we slowly begin to lose a sense for correct breathing. This makes it possible for *several centres to form,* to which we then give the names: rib- or costal breathing, clavicular, diaphragmatic or abdominal deep breathing. In all these different ways of breathing, the *point of origin of the movements* is voluntarily shifted to one of these centres. This means that each time, we are *splitting* our breathing process, which in reality is a whole, a unit, and forcing two or even more rhythms and modes of functioning on it. For the part of the whole breathing process which functions more in the entire human being, and especially through the skin, is mainly unconscious and cannot be separated easily; therefore it is held firmly to its basic rhythm. So we see: actually, we have a breathing-*organism,* which wants to function as a whole; but only one part of it, the *lung breathing-process,* can be observed. However, we do not take this fact to heart; but the part which is more accessible to the consciousness we simply regard as *the* breathing process. This is why we have been able to forget that our breathing is a living *organism.* It must obey its own inherent principles; and we cannot resist these without falling ill.

If we wish the breathing process to get well (and ourselves along with it), then we must strive to give it back its

177

naturally unified, original rhythm. This means that we *must find the single correct point-of-origin of the movements, and consolidate it under the diaphragm.*

So, clearly our task must be to work on the musculature of the diaphragm and abdomen, to make it so elastic and lively that it can follow all intentions of the breathing in singing.

The amount of work we must do for the elasticity, mobility, and reactivity of these muscles is truly considerable! It is not enough that they fully obey our consciousness, which we turned towards them with the help of the rhythmic element at the beginning of the schooling; rather, they must perform these activities so naturally that finally we no longer need give any conscious attention to them, *giving them over* wholly into the hands of the breathing process.

For this reason, these exercises must be done from the very beginning of the schooling. In the course of our work, they slowly but steadily transform the respiratory process to the point where it has become tough and elastic enough to take the initiative itself in singing, insofar as we are dealing with the physiological processes in respiration.

In the same measure as this takes place, the entire process of breathing can sink out of consciousness. It functions in an independent, 'natural' way — natural on a higher level, suited to the art. For the singer, this way of breathing means that he can totally forget... that he must breathe.

And if one brings this basic principle of the 'how' of breathing together with the melodic or harmonic elements — i.e. if one sings breath-exercises which from a musical point of view tend more towards the melodic or the harmonic — then this unified way of breathing is the ideal servant to bring the blessings of these exercises to the whole human organism. Whether we wish to influence the head-nerve man through a particular melodic element, or the middle rhythmic man through the harmonic element, or the limb-man through a certain rhythm (one could also call it beat) — we realise more and more that this unified respiration in singing is in itself a kind of source, from which health-giving forces continually flow to the whole human being.

* * * * *

Most readers of this book will surely understand at once that one cannot — should not — treat such exercises as these in detail in a written description. No matter how carefully one went about it, there would have to be mis-understandings and open questions, which would lead in turn to fresh confusions and harmful effects. These exercises must be transmitted live, in person, through direct demonstration; in no other way can they achieve what they should.

There is still one thing we would like to speak of here, since it can provide a real indication in an independent search and striving towards this goal — which we have unfortunately only touched on in an elementary way. The fact is that if we were sufficiently awake in our observing, we would be able to gain knowledge of correct respiration which would be a considerable help in resisting the decadence of this process. Why does it not occur to us to observe little children when they sing? Most healthy children, when they are still small, breathe correctly. Even if they take a breath in the middle of a word, or continue to sing while breathing in, this says nothing of the way they are *active* in the breathing process. However as the respiration process is subject to more or less the same disintegration as the tongue (see previous chapter) we must

179

try to observe it *before* the child has reached this turning-point in his development.

It is not only in children that we find correct breathing; we also find it in the adult, provided he is genuinely *healthy*. The only question is *when* we can find this correct breathing in ourselves. It is the moment when we awaken from sleep. If, instead of waking up right away, we remain peaceful, lying on our back, and simply try to hold on to the inner mood we have brought from sleep, we will discover another kind of breathing activity, different movements than those which set in as soon as we become fully awake and accompany us through the rest of the day. (Deep-sleep breathing is somewhat different, but this difference does not concern us here.)

One thing is certain: in these moments, we will not find any kind of costal breathing, but a very deep breathing in which the muscles of the abdomen and diaphragm carry out the movements.

Thus we see that in our school for uncovering the voice, we certainly must deal with the organic bases of singing; however, we may only deal with those *muscles* which come more or less within the sphere of our healthy *sense of motion*, never with any internal parts or with any part which is withdrawn from our consciousness.

And we do not treat our organism as a stupid mechanical thing, but as something living and moving, capable of learning like an independent being.

We can see from this viewpoint that sport-gymnastic methods for training these organs are useless for our purposes.

Of course no value-judgement on sport or gymnastics is meant; we only mean to say that the art and sport of our time *cannot* have anything to do with one another! For, what typifies modern sport is that it separates the organic from the soul-spiritual, thereby mechanising it. The demon of our times dissects that which must remain a living whole if it is to thrive; but we cut it up into individual complexes, which we observe and treat separately. Learning to sing, in the way we mean it here, simply has nothing whatsoever to do with any kind of mechanistic exercises. Artistic singing is a potentised interplay of spiritual, soul, and bodily functioning; yet in the performance itself, *only the creative forces* may consciously be at work.

From an anatomical and physiological point of view, we must regard the human being as a single organic entity, harmoniously membered within itself; the various organs are, as it were, the focal points of its functions. Hence there is no organic function or action that is closed in itself. And so we may also state: the human being does not sing with the larynx alone; rather, the *extended* larynx, reaching over the whole organism, is the real basis for his singing — and this is as much as to say: *the entire human being!*

Chapter Nine

CONCLUSION

The author of these lines, tired of the modern artistic world and of public activity, once expressed her frustration to Dr. Rudolf Steiner; and he, out of the inexhaustible fountain of his kindness, told her these words of reconciliation and support: If people would sing — more, and especially more correctly — there would be fewer crimes on earth.

There is a German folk saying that points to a knowledge of this truth:

Wo man singt, da lass dich ruhig nieder,
Böse Menschen haben keine Lieder.

'Where there's singing, fear no wrong,
Evil people have no song.'

This means that song — where it *really deserves the name* is simply the expression of a certain level of soul-development.

But Rudolf Steiner aimed at something deeper! He pointed to the power of song to touch and *transform our being*.

In former times, particularly in ancient and most ancient times, the singer guarded a chaste relation to his art, free of all personal interest, not to speak of inner or outer compromise. In our times, however, this kind of relation has been utterly lost, and *necessarily so:* with the progressive despiritualisation of humanity, the beauty of the tone has come more and more to be felt egoistically as the 'property' of the soul, less and less as the expression of spiritual revelation. For talented singers in our times, very few of whom are also true artists, their gift has rather become a means to satisfy ambition, to gain fame and money.

How much they have lost any independent relation to their art is best proven by their inability to form schools. To develop a school, one must have *one's own experience* of the tone-world; no theoretical knowledge will suffice. Thus we can understand that these artists, who grope about on the outside of their profession, must willingly or unwillingly spend their whole professional life in dependence on one or another school — unless, after an early onset of voice damage, they manage to find their own, original relationship to the freeing and uplifting nature of their art.

It is true for singing, just as for all human creation: that the 'what' must be considered, but even more the 'how'.

Singing is an art of rendering, a reproductive art; it is creative and productive only in the formation of schools, in the independent 'how' of tone-production. Here no one can help it, neither science nor tradition; it stands alone and must establish its own domain by itself.

However, the 'how' of a true art of singing — one suited to the present and pointing towards the future — is only revealed in those words of Rudolf Steiner quoted above. It will remain hidden from the miseducated singer, from the layman and the artistic dilettante, that besides the *musical 'how'* of singing, the *'how' of the school itself* is all-important.

Let the reader call to mind what we said in the first chapter about the difference between current methods and the uncovering of the voice; for the 'how' of uncovering the voice, as we mean this here, lies in becoming aware of a

183

reality that stands above the earthly reality, where the exalted cause of all sensible tone-manifestation works and weaves.

Thus, behind this 'how' there is an inner transformation of the human being, affecting his whole relation to life in all its manifestations, and therefore affecting his world-view in a positive sense. Religious, scientific, and artistic strivings will form an organic whole in it, mutually supporting one another.

For this reason, the 'how' of such an artistic schooling also entails the growth of a new and heightened feeling of responsibility towards the gifts one has received from God and towards the many who thirst for the beauty of song. Furthermore, the 'how' of our school — so much more important than the 'what' — also means that the tone-creation process taking place in the singer is unconsciously transferred to the listener.

And this is something of eminent importance! To be sure, here we enter an area which can be touched by outer science only in a crude and elementary way. For what it is capable of saying about vibration of the air and such things is only secondary; it barely scrapes the surface of this matter.

A mechanical representation of this — whatever a mechanical art of registration can tell us about the trans-ference of human tones to the sensory and emotional 'apparatus' of the hearer — can say nothing about the true creative processes which take place in the artist as he gives birth to song, nor anything about the subtle and intimate processes which answer them in the listener.

Spiritual science, however, enables us to know that the organs active in singing — the larynx — stand in a *close inner relation* to the listener's organs of reception — primarily the ear.

A bad speaker or singer violates not only his own organs, but also those of his audience; for the unnatural 'how' of his tone-production carries over to his hearers. Do we not often feel hoarse or cramped in the throat when we are forced to listen for a long time to a hoarse speaker, or to a singer who holds and compresses his air?

For in singing just as in other things, what is right or wrong (good or bad, appropriate or inappropriate to the times — as one will) must have wholesome or unwholesome consequences. With a speaker who makes himself ill through a wrong method, *his hearers also fall ill* in a subtle way.

And naturally, it is not the beauty of the organ that matters here; for it is quite possible to sing wrongly despite having a pleasant voice.

For some readers it may be difficult to understand this fact, especially in the concise way it has been put. This is because we are simply unaware of the consequences of improper use of the singing organs.

Why is it that in almost every case, the careers of professional singers last such a short time after they have reached their peak? It is amazing, when we consider that the same organs are used for singing as for speaking, and the power of speech generally stays with us into the most advanced age. True, in our times we have lost the consciousness for true artistic speech as well (see Rudolf Steiner's work on speech formation), and this also causes much damage; but it does not have the catastrophic effect on our laryngeal organisation and its forces which an improper activity in singing produces.

It follows from what we have said that when one *sings rightly*, the capacity to sing stays with one into old age.

And so it is! For example, it has happened not a few times that people entered this school who had never sung and were firmly convinced they had no voice, though they bore a great longing and love towards singing; and through a persistent application of these exercises, to their astonishment — and joy — *they had a voice!* And this took place despite the fact that they had past the age of forty, when the singing forces generally begin to dwindle.

It is possible to understand such phenomena only when one considers what was said at the beginning of this book. One need only remember that the voice is not an earthly thing that comes and goes and can be grasped like other material things, but a supersensible entity having an independent *existence of its own*; whether or not a person can sing outwardly — this matters little to it. And so it becomes obvious that one need only clear away all the accumulated obstacles, all the 'dams' — in short, all the damage brought on by disuse or misuse — and the stream will flow, even if for three-quarters of a lifetime one has believed one had no voice at all.

As we can see now, all the questions as to the conditions for true singing culminate in the question of the health of our singing organs. Usually we are dealing with such subtle forms and also *degrees* of the most various pathological states, that we are not aware of them ourselves; and the external medical science *must* simply be at a loss when it tries to confront them. For with such diseases, one can only find the right diagnosis, and the corresponding remedies, when one is prepared to search within the art itself. In fact, this search and remedial correction would have to begin at a time when the child is still in the process of forming his organs of speech and singing i.e. *throughout the school years!*

One has to have experienced oneself what it means when a child has always heard only proper speech and singing, and has been brought up to sing rightly himself from the beginning, in order to judge what tremendous damage is prevented thus! And it cannot be repeated often enough: quite apart from this, if a child has had such an environment and upbringing, a correct artistic education will seem just a game to him, compared with the immeasurably hard struggles and the hurdles which must be overcome by those who were not spared — who were forced in early childhood and then in school to violate their singing and breathing organs by screaming instead of singing. (See also chapter 7.) For the particularly serious aspect of these pathological states is that they do not remain confined to the larynx, but convey this degeneration directly to the rest of the human organism.

It becomes ever clearer in practice that this school for uncovering the voice represents in itself a powerful and many-sided therapeutic means. Yet it should not be hard to see that timely *prevention* of damage is to be preferred to *correction* at a later stage, the more so as it becomes ever clearer that injuries which have led to actual physical alteration can never be fully repaired.

Thus it can be seen: behind the 'how' the way we deal with the voice, there lies something of manifold significance; for it is just in this 'how' that we find what is creative in an independent art of singing.

Indeed, if there were more singing — and truer singing — in the world, as would be truly appropriate for our times, then criminality would have to decline; for all that is sick and unsuited to our times would be effectively combatted.

On many occasions, and quite consciously, we have used the expression 'an art of singing required by our times'. And perhaps someone might say: 'Well, doesn't our materialistic epoch have just the kind of singing suited to it?'

But this is not right! The age of materialism may not be over in its living effect, but it has already been overcome in its spiritual source. 'Away from materialism': this is a general, though still rather unconscious, longing of mankind. And this longing is based on lawful, though still unconscious, transformations in human nature which must precede such an expression of longing.

For the human being changes organically, physically, and psychically from epoch to epoch; and when the will to transform becomes conscious to him, he is already transformed in his unconscious.

Along with the metamorphosis of human nature, there is also a metamorphosis in singing. In different epochs it has been very different; in most ancient times, it could hardly even be compared with our present singing, and in the future it will change again. Thus the art of singing, which exists independently in itself, has to transmit the appropriate method of singing to humanity from epoch to epoch.

Just *once* a sort of exceptional condition arose: in the epoch of materialism; this should be understandable from all that we have said.

Certainly one could object, even with apparent justification, that the old schools, which never entirely lost sight of the right way, still bring forth late blossoms. This does not refer to such born singers as Jenny Lind, Patti, etc. (although they also sang under the sign of the decline), but contemporaries such as Caruso, Hempel, and Ivogün. True, it was the strength of more or less instinctive talent, and the support of mother tongue and folk-soul (Caruso, Giannini) that brought these singers to greatness, despite miseducation; still, they are late blossoms on an old tree. And we feel that the outer beauty of these late blossoms is really autumn colours — colours which are already beginning to fade in the cold of the approaching winter.

* * * * *

We have spoken of the state of our present-day art of singing as a sort of exception; but we must not forget to consider the outer circumstances, the framework within which this 'exceptional art' exists, as well as the general kind of consciousness and sensibility with which it is received in the world.

Looking objectively at the concert and opera world today — not only as a performing artist, but also as a listener — one can easily sense that these forms have outlived their time, that they are becoming empty and boring. In any case, fewer and fewer people today have a vital *need* for musical experience in this form.

It is this phenomenon alone — which is scarcely hard to recognise from the general state of affairs — that gives us the courage to attempt a new prospect, one that might well bring us into a new, deeper and more embracing relationship to these matters.

However, it is not hidden from us that in our times it must be very difficult to bring about a change of consciousness in regard to our inner and outer attitude to these things. For there is a firmly established belief that only a small fraction of young people should have the *right to choose a purely artistic calling in life.* It is felt that if someone does not show exceptional gifts from the beginning, he should leave art alone and do something 'useful' — even if all his interests, hopes and will in life point solely in this direction.

Mankind has slowly but surely forgotten that art is given *with equal right to all men* as a gift of God, that a serious involvement with some form of art is *as necessary to us as our daily bread.* But *by our day, all awareness of this has been utterly lost.*

Thus, in time, such forms as our concert and opera world have developed, where two separate principles stand crudely opposed: the actively performing artist (in its crassest form, the 'star') and the passively receiving audience (both those with true aesthetic appreciation, and those who wish to be entertained).

And so it is more than understandable that the whole world of singing is moulded by these norms, which slowly turn art into a sort of empty 'business'.

And at the same time, we inevitably lose the sense that in truth, *all and any contact* with art, whether as an artist or a so-called spectator, really has the effect of *an appeal, a plea* to the higher worlds which bestow life.

At the same time, we have likewise lost any consciousness of responsibility towards art itself!

Who knows, or has any experience of what the ancient Greeks took so seriously (though of course it cannot be repeated today in that way)? In their day, whoever dared to add a foreign tone to the so-called planetary scales, or even worse, to sing a scale belonging to another folk, was punished with death!

Of course, this attitude rested on a constitution quite different from our own, which gave the Greeks a kind of connection with the spiritual worlds that cannot even be compared with our own.

And yet, perhaps it was not necessary to forget this earnestness *so thoroughly!*

To be sure, music in particular was something quite different for the ancient Greeks than our musical art is for us. Their music was still wholly and directly connected with the spiritual worlds. The ancient Greek was still able to hear inwardly the sounding of the cosmos; he still *experienced* the harmony of the spheres, the supersensible reality in the eternal laws of music, as it has been transmitted to us under the name of Pythagoras. And with this experience, the most weighty and earnest responsibility was inextricably linked!

Since then, music itself has changed in the course of time, and human hearing has also gone through many and great changes. Through the late Greek period, the middle ages, and all the great and small stages in between — in which a Beethoven, a Bach, or a Bruckner still lived as isolated channels for musical inspiration — and on into recent times, when film music and jazz push more and more into the foreground: gradually music has fallen to earth; it has taken on the weight of the earth, and today is totally at the mercy of our wanton human wills.

Of itself it no longer steps forward to show us, or let us experience our responsibility.

And yet there are men today like Hauer (see his book on the Melos*), who feels the emptiness and unfruitfulness of contemporary music so keenly that he wishes to call it 'noise'. And he as well comes by an inner compulsion (though from quite another approach) to inward listening. And he as well calls for a new consciousness, a new attunement to the depths of artistic and musical problems.

It is true — we must come again to really spiritual music! All, all of us must gradually develop the capacity to hear the harmonies of the spheres.

For this, however, we must thoroughly transform our forces of consciousness for these wholly new aims. The development of the right sensibility or attunement provides the fundamental experience out of which the germ of this capacity can grow, so that one day the human being will be able to rediscover spiritual music. And this is the very first thing we must transform: *our whole inner and outer attitude towards everything connected with the art and art-world of today.*

---

*Joseph Matthias Hauer. 'Deutung des Melos' (The Meaning of Melos), E.P. Tal & Co. Verlag, Leipzig, Vienna, Zürich.

If we tried to put what we have said into more concrete terms, relating to the practical attitude of soul to be taken, then we would have to say:

In any serious dealing with art, we should no longer set ourselves the *aim* of being able to 'perform' certain artistic dexterities (whether innate or acquired); rather, we should only feel satisfied when, by way of properly conducted exercises, we are permitted to connect ourselves directly with the wonderful forces which stream towards mankind out of higher realms, carried on the pinions of Art. That is, we should not care so much about an 'artistic goal' set according to human estimation, as about going, or being permitted to go, on such a *path* at all. And this consciousness should be enough to spur us on to work for art earnestly, responsibly, and without self-seeking.

Then, when one has achieved a certain level of accomplishment at the end of schooling, it should be felt as a real gift; and the whole human being — thinking, feeling and will — should feel wholly indebted for it to the origin of his artistry: to a spiritual world. This means that there is no ambition or self-seeking in one's motivation, but that one is ready to see hardships and hindrances as very real indications of lacks and weaknesses in one's own human constitution, for which one summons up all one's forces to overcome and balance them.

In striving to be an artist through such an attitude, gradually real and positive forces flow into our growth as human beings: moral, social, and freedom-impulses.

Moral, insofar as we direct our active work on ourselves, against our own errors and imperfections.

And social? Here we are touching on a deep, miraculous secret; and when we experience it in its simplicity and greatness, it is certainly capable of shaking us and awakening enthusiasm: *The tone-world itself represents the archetypal motif of social life!* Truly, if we observe the way the tones behave during such a schooling, we have the most beautiful and perfect social model which human senses can perceive: they support and help one another; the first tone waits for the following, lending its forces to the weakest and last of them, until they are all ready to enter the next step of schooling together, as a unity. No matter how great and various the difficulties may be for the single tonal entities, the tendency always remains the same: to unite and carry one another, to balance each other out. And then, with such an attitude, any kind of envy or haste must appear simply senseless; so we can stand by one another as we push forward along our equally difficult paths towards a goal which means the same thing to all of us: a *true freeing of our humanity*.

And now it is time to speak about a particular fact which is inherent and unique to this school: alongside of individual work, it likes best to work with many voices together. It is not through individual instruction alone that one makes the fastest progress, but when many sing the exercises together. In listening to the others, in modestly but justly joining one's own voice into the choir of the others, in lovingly carrying the others along until the whole can blend together into one — we have something that intimately touches and promotes the development of the individual voices. Social in the deepest sense of the word!

Moreover, working in such a way, we will gain a common experience of that pure fire which can light up a knowledge of the true purpose of art in us: it is the warmth we bring up from inside through our own activity; and this warmth we need so badly, because it is the source of all life, it is regeneration and healing for our whole human nature.

Truly, when human beings are able to listen once again with reverence, in a chaste experience of art, then real enthusiasm will find access to our hearts! It will give us the strength and endurance to fight the cold, rigidifying, deadening powers which more and more wish to assert themselves out of the subhuman, the criminal.

For this is the true purpose of art and its bearers!

It is not in order to provide the human being with a refined form of amusement that music and song stream down to the earth! Rather, it is for the sake of *this* purpose that they offer themselves to us as a *sacrifice!* And this offer is for every single human being, regardless of talents or gifts.

Practising in *such* a way, if we can together experience a *knowing search* for the lost spiritual springs of music and for ways to help them be manifested again in human singing, then we can grow to be the instrument of a truly social art — which means nothing less than an art inspired by the Christ-impulse.

And when this awareness can shine through us completely, then it will gradually become possible to leave behind the old forms of musical performance — especially the crass separation between the performing 'star' and the passive listeners — and replace them with new and truly social ones.

That heaven has given us this gift, that it has created ways towards Art, on which we may purify and broaden our human nature — this is *grace!*

Truly, only he will experience it thus who is able to feel religious in the depths of his soul — as well as the true artist. Both, in their creative moments, experience the immediate reality of this higher, spiritual world, even if their experience be naive. For what is it that these two do, but to build bridges between the earthly world and the higher world?

But these bridges must be strong and sure, if they are

194

to carry across the many souls who are neither priests nor artists, yet in whom there germinates the scarcely conscious longing for salvation from the empty darkness of a materialistic world view.

Where these bridges end — this is where we can find a true science of the spirit, out of whose wide and deep realms of knowledge we can learn what we need in order to orient ourselves consciously in these higher worlds. We may call it a fact, that many who work towards art in this way find an easier access to spiritual-scientific truths. For when genuine enthusiasm has permitted us to glimpse the reality of the spiritual world, what sense is there in resisting the only science which is capable of casting light on this world and its laws?

Of course, we must live and learn what is artistic through art itself; but if we wish to *understand* what we are doing, to connect it fully with out forces of consciousness, then we have need of spiritual science, because it alone can explain the link between the creative tone-world and the deed of the singing human being.

Without a science of the spirit, for example, not even a fraction of what we have tried to present in this book would have been possible. For to experience and tell of phenomena is one thing, but to clothe them in concepts and bring them into a certain connection is quite another.

Likewise, without the kind and forthcoming help of Rudolf Steiner with the difficult problems and experiences that came up during the long period of seeking, this school certainly could not have come to the degree of relative completion it attained before this friend of humanity left the physical plane. And now, at the end of this book, it should not seem surprising if we wish to remember him again in reverent thankfulness.

Once an understanding for spiritual science has come

into the human heart, it will be found easier to understand all the things we have been describing.

New capacities will grow in the new young people in order to overcome obstacles in body and soul. Souls will be more open to the spiritual world, and will discover more and more out of themselves the things of which this schooling speaks.

When human consciousness is again fully awake to the mystery that is Man, then it will also be known that any true artistic practice must also flow into *mystery wisdom*.

It was out of the mysteries alone that the ancient Greek received spiritual music.

If we wish to achieve it again, our task must be to prepare a new mystery centre, suited to the consciousness of our times, out of the powers of our own hearts and minds. In fact we will only be able to do this if we seek these powers in spiritual science itself; it will give us the means to find the way from the coarse and sensible to the supersensible.

Perhaps what can be heard today in the sound of properly understood and mastered singing may seem just a promise; nevertheless, it is behind this promise that the real possibility of experiencing a spiritual world waits for us.

In the whole course of this book, we have come to recognise more and more that in reality, inward listening carries the key to the mystery of singing in itself. And although this book must seem scientific in the outer structure of its content, it must not be overlooked that it was the selfless devotion to a purely *artistic* ideal which provided all the impetus, courage and patience for this work. Therefore, as our last chapter, we wish to speak in a different way about this *purely artistic* principle of listening. If it is to manifest its true nature, it demands a different form of presentation: purely artistic language, arising out of creative fantasy. This is the great source on which the artist must continually call, which can bring long-forgotten truths in the human soul to consciousness and make them fruitful. And the growing singer experiences it as fruitful in the deepest sense of the word, when he becomes conscious of the forgotten sense of listening.

Thus, to conclude our book, we wish to let the sense of listening speak for itself. Let it make us the bridges by which we can turn back out of science into the world of pure art.

Motto

Ihr Sterne, Himmelszeichen
der makrokosmischen Wahrheit,
zu Lauten geronnen schenket ihr uns
Euer eigenes Wesen!

Ihr Sphären, Klangeswelten,
aus Gottes Gnade geboren,
o tönet, durchströmet uns heilig
mit reinigender Kraft!

(O Stars, heavenly signs
of macrocosmic Truth —
condensing into sounds of speech
you bring us the gift of your own being.

O Spheres, worlds of Music and Harmony
born of the Grace of God —
Sound through us, make flow through us
your holy stream of purifying power.)

Chapter Ten

ON THE FORGOTTEN SENSE OF LISTENING

In the early May morning twilight we stepped slowly down towards the valley through dew-glistening green. The last veils of mist passed, gentle and silvery, before us, bestowing numberless beads on each leaf, each blade of grass. The blossom-stars greeted us tenderly with their colours woven of light: a magic hush spread round us. Our foot scarcely moved, our breath scarcely flowed; and our heart was aware: we were entering a realm hitherto shrouded from us, where nature's deep mysteries are at work.

And as we stood there, still, sunken in ourselves, a gentle sorrow took us, as it takes the traveller who is allowed to witness a solemn ritual, but can know nothing of its deepest sense.

There — above us in the flowering tree, a small singer pipes up rejoicing. Out of the enchanted stillness, we were startled so suddenly that we could feel the beating of our hearts. Like morning bells, flight of soul, deepest devotion, it poured from the tiny throat. What solemn beauty in this deed! Oh, if but we human beings could be so wholly true and devoted!

The ache, it grew and grew in our soul; the human being envied the creature.

But in the midst of the streaming floods of song, the little bird abruptly ceased. What had happened? Did it fly away? Did we frighten it?

No, it still sat on the flowering branch — but motionless, rigid and silent. In the little creature's posture, such overwhelming tension was expressed that it seemed to penetrate into our own limbs — we stood as though spellbound.

Is it waiting? Does it see something invisible to our gaze? Intuitively we know the truth: it is listening, deeply listening to the re-sounding of its own rivers of song as they swing ever higher into the blue morning-ether. And the same holy stillness spread irresistibly over valley and hill: breathless listening, the sacrifice which nature offers to its creator. 'And man? What sacrifice does creation's highest being offer?'

The question is born in the anxious silence of our soul. 'Sacrifice? He? — Does he then know of his own true origin? Does he yet know the way to his father's house? Does he not stand exiled like a pariah, gaping and foreign, while all about him sacred revelation unfolds. To whom, then, should he bring his offering, to whom?' — Instead of an answer, our soul brought forth only yawning emptiness. And only one of those questions is yet touched, others urge forward: 'Stood I, man, always so abandoned? Was never my being bound up with yours, never intimate? But how then can pain and longing be born in me at the sight of your deed of sacrifice? — Have I drunk so deeply from the cup of forgetfulness? — Surely once I was a member of the circle of creation, surely once I swayed as a brother in the round-dance of all being?'

Then, in the deepest shaft of memory an intimation awakens, and suddenly forms itself into certainty: 'On the earthly pilgrimage you have forgotten the true origin of your being. In times now long forgotten, you also knew the bliss of sacrifice, but forgetting spread out its dark wings and covered it. — So you forgot sacrifice, you forgot listening; the dust of untruth settled upon your singing, robbed it of its cleansing power and riveted it fast to your body's heaviness.' Not so the creature. In its tiniest stirring of a muscle, there is listening. 'Will this offering of gratitude rise to the bright portal? Was the power of giving pure and holy? Or does the weight of earth lie too heavy on the wing-beats of the tones? O messengers of God, may one created by you bring his reverent offering?'

Anxious expectation in the creature. Enchanted, deeply hushed in listening, nature also asks. Expectation extends through space, becomes a being in itself, penetrating creatively into the souls of the two human listeners. The bond breaks! Unsealed, our eye gropes, our ear reaches out, the breath makes ready for a spring: 'Behold, there it comes, it comes towards us from on high!' Golden fleece yet untouched by earthly sun-rays. Out of regions which have no need of the day's star, blessing floods down mildly to earth. Heaven's gates stand opened wide! On radiant wings, beings most exalted in myriads bear blessing-power down, and their flight becomes harmonious accords! The greeting of the cosmos comes tenderly down to the little singer, lovingly dissolving his rigidity: 'Yes, your offering is heard, your listening accepted, accepted is the listening of all your brothers — take in return the gift of blessing, blessing for the earthly ground that must bear all creatures!'

But then, with primordial solemnity, almost punishing the hearing ear, there intone the words: 'Sighing under the weight of man's debt, whose darkening power was felt into the very cosmos, the earth itself once waited transfixed with pain, turning heavenwards in breathless listening: the Sun King descended to the earth-world below, o fathomless mystery! To the earth's suppressed and doleful toning HE gave new sound, and ordered it again into the ringing of the spheres. Let the earth and all creatures praise their

200

creator with their song, with their toning, for evermore — and holy is their deed. Yet their listening forms itself into a vessel; and this they hold up to the divine worlds, to receive the stream of mercy from above.

'Human being, were you not also given a voice, one whose beauty is incomparably more sublime than all the wonders you can hear on earth? Will the thought not dawn on you, that blessings of thousandfold grace wait for you, when you will find the strength to so purify your earthbound voice that through its sacred song of supplication it can reach into the spirit-realm? The will to sacrifice will point the way for it. But first, with courage seek to form the chalice, precious and pure, seek to learn hearkening, innermost listening. Hearkening's holy cup, hold it up to the starry worlds — wait in trust, until a blessing shower may fill it.' The earnest words die away. The forces of earthly heaviness engage once more in their accustomed spheres of power. Heaven's portal of grace is closed.

Awakening as out of a deep dream, our senses returned; we looked upon one another, shyly — shaken to the very bottom of our soul. Involuntarily our eye sought longingly the first ray of morning sun.

New dignity gave power to our hearts, the stream flowed through all our limbs, and slowly we began to step, turning in deep silence towards our earthly dwelling place.

Afterword

PHYSIOLOGICAL AND THERAPEUTIC
CONSIDERATIONS

Dr. Eugen Kolisko

When, in 1925, I first came to know the Werbeck-Svärdström school of singing, I was amazed to find that the method of singing and the practical exercises developed there were in total accordance with the basic physiological views developed by Rudolf Steiner on the threefoldness of the human organism. Ever since I first met this significant personality in 1914, I have dealt uninterruptedly with the physiological and medical questions posed by the human organism. The idea of threefold organisation gave me the key for solving these questions. I was also trying to find out how human artistic activity can be understood physiologically on the same basis.

In Frau Werbeck-Svärdström's school I found a kind of singing which originates wholly out of artistic sensibility. Nevertheless this art, created without any conscious reference to physiological facts, was in complete harmony with the fundamental physiology views which I had come to recognise as the correct and fruitful ones.

I then strove to live into this method completely. I took part in the general singing courses, also taking private instruction with Frau Werbeck herself, and through her friendly solicitude I had the opportunity to sit in on the lessons she gave to her students. In this way I obtained a full view of the teaching method as a whole, and also of the individual way each pupil was dealt with.

It became clear to me that the single phases of the schooling, the different singing exercises, the forming of the vowels and consonants, and also the special way of gradually separating and re-uniting the sound and speech-organisms, all proceed out of a direct and simple perception of the entire human being in his singing and speech activity. Frau Werbeck-Svärdström is wholly an artist; nevertheless, in each single exercise and its way of use, her singing embraces the same functional, spiritual-supersensible foundations which the physiologist and doctor must find if he is ever to understand the essential nature of man, and heal pathological states.

Because in this school the activity of singing is regarded as something which comes from the entire human being, not as something produced by single physical organs, it must see the human voice as something that lives in every human being, penetrates him completely, and can only be prevented from appearing by physical hindrances. It must be a school for uncovering the voice; for a schooling in singing really can only uncover and reveal that which is already present in each human being.

Therefore this kind of singing has not only an artistic effect, but also a therapeutic one. Very often there is an extraordinary increase in singing ability. Students who had no particular bent towards singing or regarded themselves as 'completely untalented' discovered capacities which had lain quite hidden. Joy in singing awoke, and obstacles in the soul life were overcome.

The same is of course true of artistic activity in general. Even where no talent at all has been apparent, it opens up undreamt-of capacities which were simply uncovered. A great number of people who suffer under ideas of inferiority and other psychological obstacles could be freed from them if these concealed, undeveloped, perhaps even atrophied artistic capabilities were cultivated in the right way. I have found this confirmed again and again, both in my practice in the Waldorf school in Stuttgart as well as in the treatment of patients.

The same thing was found in the Werbeck school of singing. The exercises had a healing effect on certain disorders of the respiratory and throat organs. Frau Werbeck-Svärdström had already noticed this in her many years of teaching, and then I came with my particular interest in this therapeutic side of singing. Together, through joint study, we developed a kind of 'curative singing' which was then applied for all different sorts of disorders. In part, singing as such was used, and in part the customary exercises were formed into special curative exercises. We were able to achieve satisfactory results with asthma, in cases of stuttering, language learning difficulties and poor hearing in children, as well as with many disturbances in organs of the throat, pharynx and nasal cavities. Naturally, this curative singing demands an exact knowledge both of the disorders and diseases as well as the effect of the exercises. This is only possible by means of an exact and well-trained collaboration between the doctor and singing teacher. Very special success was also achieved in curative pedagogy with backward children. In some of the institutes which follow the educational methods of Rudolf Steiner, curative singing has become an indispensable aid.

On the basis of a great deal of experience, it has become my certain conviction that this way of singing will also become very important in normal education for the school child.

In 1934, when Frau Werbeck-Svärdström asked me to give a course for her students on the nature and physiological bases of her school of singing, I was glad to agree. This required me to go very deeply into the essential nature of the human speech and singing organism and the principles of this school.

In this investigation it became quite clear that for an understanding of singing, as it is presented in the now complete book of Frau Werbeck, the present-day conception of the physiology of the organs of speech and singing is not quite sufficient. To be sure, an enormous amount of facts and details are known, but the one thing of fundamental importance is not considered: that singing and speech come from a higher sphere, which permeates the entire human being, and not out of the so-called organs of speech and singing. In order to understand these writings of Frau Werbeck-Svärdström, a broadened physiology of speech and singing is needed. This can be derived from the spiritual-scientific knowledge of man established by Rudolf Steiner.

Among the lectures and writings of Rudolf Steiner, extremely significant and fundamental thoughts can be found on this important chapter of knowledge, but there is no comprehensive presentation. This undoubtedly would have solved many riddles in this field; indeed, no attempt, no matter how well-meant, could ever fully replace such a presentation.

However, as I read through this work of Frau Werbeck-Svärdström, I feel compelled to attempt such a supplement to the currently accepted views on voice-physiology. And so I shall follow the request of the author and give some basic consideration on these questions here.

* * * * *

The basis of the human faculty of speech and singing actually extends much further than the so-called organs of singing and speech. The larynx, the nasal and pharyngeal cavities, the palate, the tongue, the oral cavity, lips, teeth, etc., belong to quite different systems. In the animal, for example, they serve quite different functions. Some are organs of respiration, some of digestion, and some of movement. It is the singing and speech faculty of the human being which unites these organs — functionally quite different, and anatomically altogether different — into one organism. Anatomically there is no reason whatever to think of the organs of speech and singing as a unity. They are a conglomerate; and it is the function of human singing and speaking which first makes them a unity on a higher level.

This fact alone should stop us from conceiving the origin of speech and song in terms which are too materialistic and physiological.

Then there is the further fact that an exact investigation of the process of singing and speech points beyond the narrowly defined speech-organs. We shall explain this step by step.

Along with speech and singing, we must include *hearing* and *its organ*, the *ear*. Even anatomically this ought to be clear. While such a sense-organ as the eye is relatively separate and independent, this simply cannot be said of the ear. Through the Eustachian tube, the canal which connects the middle ear with the naso-pharyngeal cavity, the ear passes directly into the region of the speech and singing organs. This connection is not only for pressure equalisation or similar external purposes, as is sometimes explained, but it establishes an immediate connection between hearing and singing or speaking — a connection which is obvious to any unprejudiced observer in a wide variety of phenomena.

Song and speech require a continual monitoring through the ear. The human being must 'listen' to himself constantly in speaking and singing in order to find the right pitch or the right nuance of speech. This happens not only from without, in the same way as the other auditory impressions reach us, but mostly from within, through the naso-pharyngeal cavity and the Eustachian tube. Every movement, every muscular activity must be consciously monitored and regulated through sense organs; and it is the ear which watches over the activity of the larynx.

On the other hand, the organs of speech and singing participate in everything we hear. When listening to a singer or to someone speaking, we will always find that our larynx and the other organs involuntarily follow, imitating the positions which the other speech or singing organ is carrying out. Thus there is really no simple, passive 'hearing' at all; the larynx and its vicinity always responds actively.

One need only think of the peculiar alteration in speech which occurs in the deaf or hard-of-hearing. Here this inner control-mechanism is lost, consequently there are changes in the vocal organisation.

The occurrence of deaf-mutism testifies vividly to the close, almost inseparable connection of ear and speech-organism. Another, most practical indication of such a relation is found in the successes achieved through Werbeck curative singing with speech difficulties and hearing disorders.

Thus we can make the basic assertion that *ear* and *larynx*, the hearing and speech or singing organisation, cannot be looked at separately. They are a unity. Our anatomy and physiology do not quite give this fact its due. This is responsible for many misunderstandings in this area.

However, the faculty of speech and singing actually extends further in the human being. The whole *respiratory system* stands in a most intimate relation both to *hearing* as well as to *singing* and *speaking*. Hearing takes place by means of the air; the tone is conveyed through vibrations of the air. But this is only the outer part of the hearing process. Air also enters the human being through breathing; and this in-breathing has further effects. By expanding the chest cavity, it makes the diaphragm go down. This compresses the abdominal cavity, creating a pressure on the abdominal vessels which is then conveyed in turn to the fluid of the spinal column (cerebro-spinal fluid) and thence to the brain, where it causes an increase in pressure and a slight displacement of the brain forwards and upwards. In expiration the process is reversed: the pressure is released and the flow goes downwards. The cerebral fluid, however, is connected with the labyrinth fluid of the ear, so that the after-effects of inspiration and expiration call forth a rise or fall of pressure in the brain region as well as in the ear. Thus, while the air entering our ear as the physical vehicle of the tone is connected with the whole air-column at work in the respiratory process, this above-to-below process corresponds to another process — in the fluid of the spinal column, brain, and sense organs — which goes through the entire human being from below upwards. These two processes meet in the human being.

The hearing process is connected with all of this. In hearing, the soul element comes to meet the physical. The changes in the 'air column', caused from without, are met by corresponding changes in the 'water column'. If only the air were present, the tone would have a physical vehicle, but the soul would have no organ to receive and experience it. Hearing takes place not through the isolated ear, but through a sympathetic movement of the entire breathing-organism, insofar as this is connected with the cerebral fluid and its fluid column. This explains the remarkable fact that demonstrably deaf people do have an ability to

distinguish tones and even different kinds of music. They
say that they can 'hear' and distinguish the music with their
'back'. What happens is that the cerebro-spinal fluid, along
with the spinal cord and its nerves, acts as an extended
organ of hearing. But even in the normal human being,
hearing comes about not only through the ear, but through
the sympathetic vibration of the 'water column' in harmony
with the breathing process; and as we know this fluid flows
through and around the nervous system and the ear. In
hearing, the soul is based in the watery element, while
from without it receives the airy element on which the
tone 'sits'. All respiratory processes, however, are connected
with feelings. The feeling soul is connected with the
respiratory and circulatory system and not with the nervous
system, as Rudolf Steiner has shown with great insight.* In
breathing, the soul actually hears the tone through the
whole body, as it brings the fluid column into sympathetic
vibration with the breathing. Thus, *hearing* is connected
with the *circulation of cerebro-spinal fluid*.

Every sensory process rests on an experience of
difference between the processes which are set off in the
organism from without and the quite different processes
which come to meet these outer effects from within. Thus
in the sensation of warmth, outer warmth encounters
inner warmth; in the sensation of light, the outer light
coming in through the eye encounters a modified inner light
which comes to meet it. Rudolf Steiner put forth this
important law of psycho-physiology in 1919, establishing

* Rudolf Steiner, *Von Seelenrätseln* (Riddles of the Soul), 1917,
Dornach, Switzerland. (Excerpts in *The Case for Anthroposophy*,
ed. Owen Barfield. Rudolf Steiner Press, London, 1970.) Here it is
shown that all feeling has its bodily basis in processes of the rhythmic
system, e.g. respiration.

it with many examples.* In the case of hearing, the effect of the tone comes in by way of the air, while the soul lives within in the rhythm of the watery element; in the encounter of air and water vibration, the musical experience lights up in the whole rhythmic man. In the ear itself we find the same juxtaposition: the *labyrinth fluid* in the inner ear against the air in the outer and middle ear.

The connection of singing and speech as such with the breathing organisation is practically obvious.

* * * * *

It is chiefly respiratory organs which have transformed into organs of singing and speech. However, it is not so that the larynx and the other vocal organs are set in motion by the air, but the reverse: the activity of singing and speech makes use of air in order to express, to manifest itself. Breathing as such serves vitality, the mere maintenance of life. It is an animal process. In singing and speech, part of this process is overcome. A higher life forms out of this. Through the organs of singing and speech, the soul-spiritual forms the air of the breathing apparatus into an 'ensouled' air-organism, which then comes forth and expresses itself as song and speech. The air does not move the larynx; rather, the larynx, stimulated into movement by the soul, forms the air. Thus we can see singing and speech as a transformed breathing process which radiates through the whole body.

So, while the hearing process is carried further — through the respiratory system in inhalation — to the cerebro-spinal

* Rudolf Steiner, Lectures held in 1919 in the free Waldorf School of Stuttgart; *First Scientific Lecture Course — Light Course*, Steiner Schools Fellowship, 1977.

210

fluid and the nervous system, the singing and speech process is conveyed through the muscle to the process of exhalation, transforming the air stream into an 'air organism' permeated with spirit and soul.

Hence in the upper organism of the human being we find an *interpenetration of hearing with singing and speech*.

In the middle organism there is a connection both of the hearing process as well as the singing and speech process with the breathing.

We still must speak of the third region into which the activity of singing and speaking flows. This is the region of movement and limb activity. We said at the beginning that the process underlying speech and singing extends much further than the organs of speech and song. Even hearing actually has a tendency to flow over into movement. This is why music acts so powerfully on the organs of movement in simple people; and it explains the link between music and dance. Finally, the speech process, in gesture, also moves into the limbs.

In order better to understand the relation of voice and speech activity to bodily movement in general, we must widen our view:

Though the muscle system of the larynx is of course a part of the general muscular system, it also stands apart from it quite independently. General bodily movements come about as the impulse from the muscular system is conveyed to the skeleton, bringing the limbs or limb-like parts into motion. These then take effect in the outer world through mechanical action. In the larynx and the other organs of singing and speech, we have a system of muscle and cartilage which transfers its extraordinarily subtle movements to the air of the breathing apparatus and gives it form. While with general bodily movement the limbs of the body — and through them objects of the outer world — are moved, the activity of speech and singing sets in movement a subtle limb system, whose action moulds the exhaled air.

The far-reaching importance of this side of speech and singing has been recognised far too little. All tones, each vowel, each consonant, produce definite vibration-forms in the exhaled air. The air column inside the human being, as well as the air flowing out, takes on very exact, characteristic forms. They can even be registered or drawn by means of certain apparatuses. In this process, the human being makes use of the entire range of movements at his disposal and transfers them to the air. Sir Richard Paget, in his book *Human Speech*, gives a highly interesting presentation of these different characteristic air-column forms for each tone, vowel and consonant.*

The general movement system produces movements: these movements serve motion of the body and work in the outer world. However, all movements can also be conceived as gestures. In this sense the movement system speaks a 'silent language'. The muscle system of the larynx and of the organs of speech and singing as a whole is a highly specialised organism. It represents a sort of miniature of the muscle and bone or cartilage system of the entire body.

The same activity which plays itself out physically, and dumbly serves bodily motion, is turned inward in singing and speech: it plays on the miniature movement system of the larynx, differentiates the movement of the exhaled air of the whole respiratory system, and finally manifests itself in the musical sound of singing and the speech sounds of language. While in bodily movement the soul plays itself out more on the physical level, it

* R. Paget, *Human Speech*, Kegan Paul, London 1930.

sounds through song and speech directly and reveals its own self. The human movement organism is ensouled and then manifested again outwardly in the exhaled air as speech and song.

And this explains why speech is always accompanied by gestures. The limb system, as if aware of its original function of dumb, gestural speech, accompanies speech itself with gesture-language.

In the art of *eurythmy* initiated by Rudolf Steiner, the inner movement which lies hidden and contracted in the speech process is transmitted outwards again to the limb system. The transformed, subtle movement tendencies lying in song and speech are thus revealed in the movement of the whole human body.

The physiology of speech and singing should deal first of all with this fundamental truth. This gives us three stages:

1) Human being in motion (general muscle system);
2) Speaking and singing human being (larynx and speech organs):
3) Human being in eurythmic movement (where the inner nature of speech and singing expresses itself in outward movement).

The first stage is movement of the body. The second reveals the soul directly. The third manifests the movement of the soul in bodily motion, through a spiritual process.

We have shown how the speech and singing process passes into the general movement processes of the limb system. It first arose through an internalisation of the latter, and still uses it as the general foundation for its activity.

The speech and singing activity is thus a living process which extends in three stages through the entire human organism. Ear and larynx, with the voice and speech organs between them, form the upper member; the total breathing

213

process with its ramifications above and below forms the middle; and the processes of bodily limb movement form the lower member of this process. Speech and singing does not come from a separate organic system in the human being, but comprehends the entire person, who hears, sings, and speaks, and also expresses himself in movement.

Thus the three regions are:

1) Ear and larynx together.
2) The breathing activity and its continuation upwards and downwards.
3) General body movement.

Thus the whole human being sings and speaks.

Up to this point, we have treated speech and song as one unit. And this is quite justified; for the two have a common source. The further one goes back in the history of language, the more speech also contains the element of song. *The 'original language' is a singing speech or a speaking singing.* Only later do song and speech differentiate out of this original unity. Nevertheless the two elements were already present from the beginning as formative factors in the process of speech and singing.

These two elements are the *musical-singing* element and the *speech-sound* element.

In its development, language has tended to move away from the musical. The prose speech of modern man is the culmination of this process. The musical elements, and at the same time the poetic ones, have been excluded, and 'mere speech' has separated from the element of song.

Let us look at the singing and speech organism as it differentiates in these two directions:

The source of speech and song is located in the larynx. Though the singing and speech process embraces the entire human being, the *larynx* is the point around which it *revolves*, in order to manifest itself as speech and song.

What has formed the human being in his movements, out to the extremities of his limb system, here is manifested in its inner nature. Now the speech and singing process unfolds from the larynx out towards the head through the adjoining organs of respiration.

The windpipe continues into the nose. The organs of the oral cavity, the palate, tongue, teeth, lips, etc, actually belong to the digestive system and are put into the service of speech. The tongue, lip, and whole facial musculature develop an outward-directed limb activity intimately connected with speech.

So we have three stages in the make-up of the speech organs:

1) *Larynx*,
2) *Respiratory tract* (larynx, naso-pharyngeal cavity, nose and sinuses),
3) *Oral cavity* and associated musculature.

The further we move on this path from inside to outside, the further we leave the musical-song element behind us and come into the element of mere speech, of the speech-sounds.

The respiratory and digestive organs taken into service by the singing and speech process can be seen as instruments used by the singing and speaking human being to form and shape the intoned musical stream which flows directly from the soul. This is how the *vowels* and *consonants* arise. In the former, the musical element is still clearly felt. The form of the cavity through which it flows gives the vowel its particular colouration. A (ah) is the musical stream as it is formed passing through the vocal cords in the larynx. E is formed where the stream coming from the windpipe crosses with the pharynx, I at the back of the nose, O in the oral cavity, U where the oral cavity passes out to the outside, etc. Thus, in the vowels the

215

musical stream adapts to the shape provided by the larynx and its associated organs.

In the consonants, the plastic element finally comes into its own; tongue, palate, lips, teeth, etc., model the voice stream, and the musical element is hidden in the different consonants, even if it continues to ring softly through them.

Thus we come to the following division:

1) Musical element (larynx, voice),
2) Vowels (a musical element is present here),
3) Consonants (the formative speech-sound element is dominant).

The voice has its origin in the musical element. Moving forward, it gives itself to be formed by the speech-sound element. In this way the voice is formed into the speech sounds.

The voice itself, however, belongs entirely to the musical domain. In speech it is strongly united with the speech sounds, but much less so in singing. In fact, the voice itself really lives 'behind' its manifestation in speech sounds, in its own sound element. The musical sound stream of the voice is connected with the respiratory system. It operates in those connections which the respiratory system establishes with the nervous system, as it carries over the breathing rhythm to the movements of the cerebro-spinal fluid. There is a kind of inner 'singing' present *before* combination takes place with the speech element. Through the intoning of the larynx, this inner singing becomes outer reality. Then the voice finds outer support in the breath, climbing up and down 'vertically'. The direction to the speech-sound, on the other hand, goes 'forward'. The sound stream has a vertical direction, and holds itself towards the back. The soul experience at the same time is based on the movement of the cerebro-spinal fluid, which moves to the rhythm of the breath. If one tries to follow this process inwardly, to listen to oneself or others singing, one comes to the experience of a stream penetrating the entire human being, concealing itself behind the outer instrument and at the same time making use of it. This archetypal phenomenon can be called the *sound stream*. The living process which takes place between breathing and nerves is the real field of singing. In this, the larynx is only a kind of stimulation centre, out of which the physical voice then comes. The larynx does not produce singing any more than the heart produces blood circulation. The latter is present in the developing embryo long before the heart itself, and it is only in this circulation that the heart comes into being. Present-day researches in the field of circulation and heart physiology have long since come beyond the view that the heart is a pump. It is a regulation and perception organ in the circulation and for the circulation of the living blood. In the same way, the larynx is a delicate organ for regulating and moulding the air. Behind it, and chronologically before it, is something else: the life of the soul in the inner sound stream, which penetrates the whole respiratory and nervous process. The breathing and nerve organisation, the air and water rhythm, 'sound' together; the soul listens to this process, and at the same time actively brings the air to sounding.

Thus there is a *sound organism* situated more towards the back; in front of it, the organs of speech form a *speech-sound organism*. Both organisms are at work in singing as well as in speech. Rudolf Steiner treats this topic comprehensively. However, song arises from the sound stream, which ascends along the vertebral column to the head and ears and descends the same way, while speech is turned *forward*. Thus on the one hand it finds a relation upwards to the thought, which brings forth the *meaning* of the

217

word, and on the other hand it is connected downwards to the *limb movement,* the sculpting gesture (especially in the consonant).

In speech, we are pressed completely into the outer world. In singing, we turn back to the musical current. However, another factor has entered in: singing has incorporated aspects of speech as it has directed its consciousness too strongly away from the actual musical element towards that of the speech-sound. And on the other hand, language has taken a singing element into its consciousness which has obscured a full consciousness of the speech sounds and their sculptural power.

In singing, above all a consciousness of the sound organism as such must be found again. This is the starting point of Frau Werbeck's school. It strives to develop the sound organism. For this reason, it begins by separating singing from the speech-sound elements, to let the musical as such come through. The resulting experience — Frau Werbeck describes it in the book — can be exactly understood when we recognise the physiological foundations of breathing and hearing as we have described them. After this, it consciously takes the path of reuniting itself with the word elements, the vowel and consonant, and step by step incorporating the speech-sound organism into singing. Gradually the whole speech organism — and with it the general organism — is also brought into the singing activity, so that finally the entire human being is singing.

The art of speech formation must go the reverse path. It starts with the consonant, brings in the vowel, and finally it makes the whole of mastered speech into a musical entity on a higher level, after it has first removed unconsciously penetrating singing elements.

Such a form of singing corresponds to the physiological foundations which are in fact there. It seeks to develop

218

what is hidden in every 'voice'. In this there lies a therapeutic force as well. The simple fact of going back to the sound stream, to the sensible-supersensible element of the singing organisation, has a healing effect. People become aware that musical powers are already present in them, and that they can develop them themselves. With children who suffer from hearing or speech difficulties, simply being part of a choir of this kind will have a curative action, because they are taken along with the stream, and develop, or uncover their voice through imitation.

What Frau Werbeck-Svärdström describes in this book as stages in singing training can be related, both as a whole and in particular, to the basic ideas presented here. Both the sound organism as well as the speech organism are found to have three stages, and all phases and exercises indicated go back to the same principle. They are simply derived from an inner perception of the real, spiritual bases of singing. But they are also in accordance with the physiological facts presented here.

By way of conclusion, I would like to express my hope that this work might be received with attention in wide circles. It is a first, noteworthy attempt to structure the art of singing in accordance with a spiritually oriented knowledge of man.

TRANSLATOR'S NOTE

A few basic terms used in this book require comment or explanation: The author speaks of the 'school of uncovering the voice' (*die Schule der Stimmenthüllung*). It is significant that it is not a method, but a particular 'school' of singing; hence this word is retained in the English.

A fundamental distinction is drawn between *Klang* and *Ton* on the one hand, and *Klang* and *Laut* on the other:

Klang we must render as 'sound'; but the German word has the connotation of musical, sonorous, or at least 'non-chaotic' sound.

Ton: this refers to a musical note or 'tone'. The latter has been chosen because, like the German, it can also refer to the 'world of tone', and because the word 'note' can draw our attention to the written note.

Laut: this word we render as a 'sound of speech' or 'speech sound' (a vowel or consonant). We avoid speaking of 'a sound' in most cases, to prevent confusion with (musical) sound, i.e. *Klang*. The author also speaks of the 'word' or 'textual element' which is composed of speech sounds.

The German prefix 'ur-' we have chosen to render as 'archetypal': *Urklang* is the 'archetypal sound', *Urstimme* the 'archetypal voice', *Urbild* an 'archetype', etc.

Vorstellung is translated as a (mental) picture; *Vorstel-*

220

lungskraft as the 'power of mental representation'.

The author speaks of the 'tone-entelechy' or 'tone-being'. The latter has been used throughout; for it has a clear meaning to English-speaking readers, unlike the term entelechy.

What we refer to as 'attentive', or 'expectant', or 'inward listening' renders the untranslatable *lauschen.*

The Vowel Sounds

The vowel sounds A, E, I, O, U, Ö, Ü are to be pronounced as in German (also the consonants referred to, e.g. *ch* as in Scottish 'loch'). The German vowel sounds are pure, not diphthongs as in English; approximate equivalents would be:

A as in father
E as in faith
I as in seed
O as in so
U as in mood
Ö as in heard (British pronunciation) or French peu
Ü as in suit (British pronunciation) or French du

The author also refers to certain Scandinavian sounds:

Y (in German it could be expressed ÜJJ) — a very high Ü
Å approximately as in English awe
O as in English book, but rounder and narrower
U more closed than the German U, but no so sharp as the Ü

Further Reading by Rudolf Steiner:

Creative Speech
The Nature of Speech Formation

Eurythmy as Visible Music

Eurythmy as Visible Speech

The Inner Nature of Music and the Experience of Tone

Knowledge of The Higher Worlds
How is it Achieved?

Occult Science
An Outline

Theosophy
An Introduction to the Supersensible Knowledge of the World and the Destination of Man